PIECES OF THE PIEDM

THE PUZZLE OF

ONE L FE

A Personal Geography From Virginia's Foothills and America's Historic Heart

Essays by
WALTER NICKLIN

Illustrations by
TUCKER HILL

To Mary Winston Davis, Miriam McCullough, and Thomas Randolph 526/2,000

Library of Congress
Catalog Card number 97-77560

Nicklin, Walter
Pieces of the Piedmont,
The Puzzle of One Life: A Personal
Geography from Virginia's Foothills
and America's Historic Heart.

Monotype illustrations
© 1997 by Tucker Hill

ISBN 1-885937-06-7

CONTENTS

FOREWORD

"Write what you know," is the old dictum. To which the essayist Annie Dillard, who got her writing start by looking closer than anyone else ever had at a small creek in southwestern Virginia, has responded and honed: "Write what you *uniquely* know."

For me, that is Virginia's northern Piedmont. Most of my life, when I've written, I've done it for money. That means writing what others want — editors, their perceived audience, and advertisers who pay the bills. When I write what I want, I always find myself back home in the Piedmont.

While there must be a market for such stories — some earlier versions of which have appeared in national newspapers and magazines, where, yes, I got paid — it surprises me that more is not written about the Piedmont. How can critically acclaimed volumes be devoted to other, historically less interesting, even aesthetically bleak, parts of America, with so little put to paper specifically evoking the beautiful Piedmont, in many ways the nation's historic heart?

I suspect I know the answer: Although fixed geographically, the Piedmont is in many ways a shifting, fluid place, not lending itself to rigid categorization or genre. The rolling hills themselves seem wave-like and elusive; the history of these hills is also marked by movement and transition, of passing through, of the transmuting of the first European settlements and Old World attitudes into the American destiny and dream — the promise that lay just beyond the next hill. Today, neither ruggedly wild nor layered with a built environment, no longer traditionally rural but still free of most veneers of what passes for civilization, the Piedmont defies reductionism and definition.

The Piedmont's resistance to easy explanation is, come to think of it, not unlike trying to make sense of the accumulated, quotidian, taken-for-granted details of a person's constantly but usually slowly changing life. The Piedmont is too comfortably familiar, not unsettlingly different or dramatic; we just assume we already know all there is to know about it. With its landscape of Founding Fathers' homes and Civil War battlefields long ago embedded in the consciousness of a nation, it's not news. Or, maybe as its residents prefer to believe, the Piedmont is simply too beautiful to put into words. Or, as with any life that's lived, words will never do it justice.

But I have, in this collection of personal essays, tried. That, after all, is the root definition of an essay — to try.

I dedicate this work to my mother and her mother, who were born and reared, lived their lives, and died in the Piedmont. And to their namesakes, my two daughters, who, although now gone away to school far up north, will never forget their Virginia roots, I hope. To my tolerant wife and our new baby boy, I say thank you. And to friends and colleagues, whom I won't embarrass by naming, I am most grateful for spurring me ever onward.

THAT PECULIAR PLACE CALLED HOME

MURDER is not yet random here. There is motive, still; there is passion, simmering just beneath the surface of the softly rolling, thinly populated, slumberously peaceful landscape of Virginia's northern Piedmont, my once and present home. Even I, whom I like to think of as a rational and gentle man, have felt such spleen, I'm shamed to say, that when recalled, now 20 years later, still makes the blood rush.

It has to do with the land. There's something about the land here.

Yes, I could have killed him. A figure of speech, that's not. I didn't just wish he'd go away — a kind of death — I literally could have killed him. That is, I not only entertained the possibility but actually prepared for the fatal confrontation. It would be self-defense, of course. That's what I told myself as I shopped for a gun. Compared to this, the Army's Basic Training, where I had learned to fix bayonets and yell "Kill!," was a mere abstraction.

The urge was as real as the land itself, that freshly hayed field in the shadow of the Blue Ridge, over which the conflict had erupted. Part of my property was his and he intended to erect a new fence to prove it, the neighbor I hardly knew suddenly announced one day. Actually, he didn't use words; he simply began to uproot the old fence, whose rotting posts and rusting wire had unaesthetically but effectively delineated the respective plots for previous owners. A stack of newly cut, pressure-treated lumber, together with a post-hole digger, intruded a good 15 feet onto *my* side of the old fenceline. Like Jimmy Carter, feeling betrayed by the Soviet invasion of Afghanistan a few months earlier, I didn't know how to react. So I laughed, in the best conflict-avoidance tradition, when I finally asked:

"What are you doing?"

"What does it look like I'm doing!" He didn't laugh.

"There must be some misunderstanding," I said the obvious.

"The only one misunderstanding round here is you." A bear of a man, he stared at me until I blinked. A new fence was needed, I gathered, to hold in his livestock; and while he was at it, he might as well fix the fenceline "right." Almost a full acre of land, I calculated, was at stake.

"Well," I said, "we'll just have to check it out at the County Clerk's Office."

"You do that." And then he went back to work.

When, the next day, I brought him photocopies of all the relevant recorded deeds and plats, he wouldn't even look at them. Instead, he made a great show of working on the fence, as he paced the distance between posts, ripped down entangling vines, did everything, that is, except actually build a new fence. But over the next few weeks, as his untouched pile of new lumber itself became overgrown with honeysuckle, I began to notice that my own power tools and other possessions were mysteriously disappearing from what was supposed to be my property. Escalating acts of vandalism followed.

There was nothing I could do except report the violations (and my suspicions) to the Sheriff's Department, according to my local lawyer, who, as the reputed county boss, knew all there was to know about such things. "Not much we can do, either, under the circumstances," said a deputy, who in his resigned impotence sounded like a UN peacekeeper.

Then there was that day when my wife, working in our garden near the disputed property line, heard gunshots fired over her head. They came from the treeline along the old fence. Then came a disembodied voice: "Just trying to get that groundhog. You don't want him to tear up your garden, do you?" Then laughter rolled across the field after her as she ran.

I'll never forget that day, unusually cool and damp for a Piedmont summer. But I also remember thinking — my own attempt at laughter, I suppose — how hot and molten the field's ubiquitous rocky outcroppings must have been in their creation, long before there was any such thing as emotion, much less any such notion as presumptuous as ownership of the land. Millions of years later, now walking the disputed property line, I scooped up a handful of dust. Clinched by my fist, quickly and involuntarily, the soil became a compressed, dirty ball. I let it drop and wiped my hands on my khakis. Blood is easier to remove than the Piedmont's red clay stain, I remember thinking. And sure enough, not too long afterwards, a man, not this man but another, was shot dead off his tractor only a few miles from this spot in a right-of-way dispute. The killer, never prosecuted, claimed his victim was trespassing.

I don't know what's more perilous: fighting with neighbors or writing about them. My landgrabbing adversary has long since moved away, but I still call the Piedmont home; without the benefit of exile, I should be wary about what I say. Already I've possibly said too much — or not enough. What you've written may well be true, I can hear friends and neighbors chide, but surely a bit overwrought, don't you think? And others, as if it's the morning after I've recklessly self-indulged, will no doubt banish me with silence — at least for a day or two, to put me in my place. This is all part of the social dynamic of the Piedmont.

Having grown up here, I should have known better than to have got all worried and worked up about a fenceline feud — much less then gone and written about it. The man was just ornery, that's all. Like a lot of people around here. Hardly worth writing about, thereby sensationalizing. It happens all the time: land disputes, hunters trespassing, the crazy sound of random gunfire, odd acts of vandalism, even barn burnings and livestock poisonings. No, that's not quite right, either — sounds too much like the Wild West.

Let's just say you have to live here — better yet, be born and reared here and never move away — to understand. Having lived and worked too long in that nearest faraway place of the Northern Virginia suburbs, I had forgotten how peculiar the Piedmont is. A native now returned, I find my position, too, peculiar. Why am I here, come back home? Indeed, why do people who have the means to live anywhere in the world — Yankee industrialists, Manhattan investment bankers, Hollywood stars, retired diplomats from abroad — also choose to "come home" to the Piedmont? I'm writing to find the answers, to understand what it is about the land here, what it is that's particular to this place called the Piedmont.

Piedmont: It's a funny, foreign word, its simple yet suggestive combination of soft and hard sounds seductively enticing. But the exact nature of that seduction — the yearnings that "Piedmont" arouses — remain vague, much like the gentle land itself, whose rolling hills blend into one another. They lack the angular clarity of places like the Rocky Mountains, the jagged coast of Maine, or certainly a downtown city block. The land here has produced no *PrairyErth* or other paean, nothing to clarify the region like Faulkner's Deep South, Frost's New England, or Thomas Coles's Hudson River Valley. Yet the Piedmont exists on the map of Americans' minds, even those who've never been here; I know because of the knowing nods I've gotten over the years whenever I've told people where I'm from.

"Where're you from?" In the transient, work world of Washington, that's probably the second most frequently asked question. Often not posed directly with words but, rather, with an inquisitive glance, a discerning ear, it's a gentle, friendly interrogation — not so adversarially aggressive as that most asked question, "What do you do?" More than an attempt to pigeonhole or label, the "hometown" question is, I think, a genuine attempt to understand who you are. For if there is a core to a human being beyond cells and tissues and guts, and if it can be identified beyond fussy words like "soul," it must surely evoke a particular place, a reflection of the external landscape where one was born and raised. The question, then, is a way to seek connections, common ground. It's the environmental side of nature-versus-nurture personality development, not microscopically abstract like genes. "Where you're from?" is something solid we can put our hands on, like the earth itself.

But I wonder if people's images of a place, in this media age, are ever a true mirror of one's self. Just because I'm from the Piedmont doesn't mean I spend most of my days in jodhpurs and hobnob with the likes of Patricia Kluge, Robert Duvall, or Paul Mellon. For that's the popular image of the Piedmont: an indefinitely located region of historic Virginia, somewhere west and sort of south of Washington, where old and new money meet as country gentry. People conjure up Middleburg, with its shoppes like in Nantucket, maybe the Hamptons. Or Charlottesville, home of Thomas Jefferson, lots of literary types in corduroys and tweed jackets with elbow patches, and *The* university for Virginia gentlemen. Somewhere in between, in the absolute middle of nowhere, there's some place

called Rappahannock with its world-renowned, five-star restaurant, The Inn at Little Washington. Proliferating vineyards and wineries, like Civil War battlefields, are everywhere, but most people stick to what they already know, good old bourbon.

These images aren't entirely wrong, but they're not altogether right, either. So what exactly is the Piedmont? A literal definition, though easy enough, only scratches the surface, physiographic and otherwise: The Italian *Piemonte* means "foot of the mountains." Thus the Appalachian foothills were named by early settlers, as they often did, after something they already knew: in this instance, the gently rolling landscape found in much of Europe. This part of Virginia wasn't such a strange, foreign land after all; it reminded them of where they'd come from. English country homes and their accompanying lifestyle were all that was missing.

What geologists call a peneplain, the Piedmont is a plain not yet worn completely smooth by inevitable erosion. East to west, the Piedmont begins where the flat coastal plain ends, clearly delineated by the rivers' fall lines. Here the broad, tidal estuaries narrow, at rapids and waterfalls, into true rivers — fresh water flowing continuously downstream. This was as far upriver as ocean-going ships could travel and as far downriver as cargo could cross without need of a ferry. And so it was on the fall line, a classic case study in geographic determinism, that early centers of commerce naturally developed: Alexandria and

Georgetown on the Potomac, Fredericksburg on the Rappahannock, Richmond on the James. "The West" was then the Piedmont, the first frontier. Beyond, where the sun set, the impenetrable mountains.

Although the Piedmont region stretches along the Eastern Seaboard from New York City to Montgomery, Alabama, few but Virginians and Carolinians are likely to use the word "Piedmont" with any fluency. It's a cartographer's term, a geographical handle, a history tool to understanding of early American settlement. Less sure, more complicated, is what lies beneath the surface, what caused the Piedmont's defining topographic features.

So-long-ago geological origins, like forces that shape the self, cannot be observed directly, only inferred. The serene landscape of today's Piedmont gives little hint of its cataclysmic beginnings; but its hot, humid, dripping-wet summer days — which my grandmother, rocking on the front porch and fanning herself, called "close" — are suggestive. As are the rolling hills themselves, conjuring up fluid motion, even waves. And the sometimes heavy haze hanging on the distant but ever-present mountains, like seashore fog. For water once covered what would become the Piedmont, lapping against the shore where the Blue Ridge now stands.

This ancient sea is called the Iapetus. All that remains from that time, 600 million years ago, is metamorphosed sandstone from the clean, white beaches. Driving on Interstate 66 past the aborted site of Disney's theme park, you can see this white quartz capping the Bull Run mountains — or monadocks, the geological term for the hard, resistant rock surmounting a peneplain. The rest of the Piedmont's Paleozoic past was obliterated when the earth's shifting crustal plates squeezed North America and Africa together 300 million years ago. The enormous force of the continental collision, coupled with the hot friction of the land masses grinding together, thrust upward the Piedmont and Blue Ridge, whose then towering Alp-like rocky layers toppled over to form, as folded remnants, the Appalachian ranges to the west.

This mountain-building event is known as the Appalachian Orogeny. That's easier to remember than the names of faces from my youth, whom I sometimes think I see now, changed and hardened like metamorphic rock: Standing in line at the Post Office or at the new Giant superstore, we smile and nod, yet we're not sure we're who we think we are. We don't dare fumble for first name greetings. Because we did not grow old together, we might as well be dead, with youthful images of each other fossilized like trilobites that once swam the Iapetus Sea.

But unlike faces and bodies, the earth here ages well.

There are lots of ways to understand the earth, to look at the land: The Puritans saw evil in the harsh weather and unconquered wilderness. Their Yankee descendants, the Transcendentalists, saw God. But in the South, particularly the gentle, temperate Virginia Piedmont, the land has always offered up the opportunity for lives well lived. God was implicit in nature, all right, but it was a God illuminated through reason — not through revelation. This God was Farmer, Builder, and Architect. By following His example and making your own mark on the land, your life itself was deified. This was the Deism professed by that ultimate Piedmont man, Thomas Jefferson, whose name is always invoked in debates about the Piedmont's future.

For now, the Piedmont lies largely in the past. The land still seems to belong to those who first settled here and named it — in itself a God-like act. History lives in every placename, each with its individual story to tell, even the jurisdictional entities. Of the nine counties that comprise the Virginia's northern Piedmont, four were named after Colonial Governors (Albemarle, Culpeper, Fauquier, Loudoun), two after a British prince (Orange) and princess (Louisa), two in honor of Revolutionary heroes (Madison, Greene), and one Indian tribe (Rappahannock). The names of the Piedmont's grand estates tell of FFVs (first Families of Virginia) — Leeton Forest and Carter Hall — and of lives lived in comfortable harmony with nature — Berry Hill, Greenwood, Ash Lawn. (Even the old house where I live, retains its name — Paradise — from the days before its farm acreage was sold off. When Union soldiers camped here during the Civil War, the name of Paradise was changed temporarily to Bleak Hill.)

As much as any words can, these placenames evoke the land they christened. For the Piedmont remains in many respects just as the settlers, these namers, shaped it: tiny crossroads villages; lonely manor houses and outbuildings; cultivated fields and grazed pastures, whose boundaries are precisely fixed by dry stone walls or post-and-board fencing; second-growth timber, from scraggly cedars to a rich assortment of hardwoods and scrubs. This land was ideal for working to man's will, but the ubiquitous hills — undulating westward, ever steeper, like sensuous swells, until they crest in the Blue Ridge, where the Piedmont ceases — could never be flattened. Not by man anyway, not even today's bulldozers; only forces as ineluctable as erosion could ever flatten the hills; and by then, we and our descendants will no doubt all be dead. Until then, the landscape would be as recognizable to Alexander Spotswood as it was to me, when I returned home. He was the Royal Governor who, in 1716, together with a dozen other aristocratic colonials (known to every Virginia schoolchild as the "Knights of the Golden Horseshoe") ventured into what was then the frontier and opened the Piedmont to colonization.

"We drank the King's health in champagne and fired a volley — the Princess' health in Burgundy and fired a volley, and all the rest of the Royal Family in claret and fired a volley. We drank the Governor's health and fired another volley. We had several sorts of liquors, viz., Virginia red wine and white, Irish usquebaugh, brandy, shrub, two sorts of rum, champagne, canary, cherry, punch, cider, etc." So wrote a member of Spotswood's festive and gaily dressed party upon crossing the Piedmont and reaching the top of the Blue Ridge — then baptizing the Shenandoah River on the other side as "the Euphrates."

Almost 250 years later, the drink, though now of course mostly bourbon, still flows. And though no rifle volleys are heard, there are plenty of toasts: Ding, dong, the Mouse is dead! For this particular party is a benefit ($150 per head) dance for the Piedmont Environmental Council (PEC), which led the fight against the Disney America theme park. Many of the men are dressed in the scarlet of foxhunting attire, fashionably matching their flushed checks, while the women's evening gowns are as understatedly alluring as the lush landscape they're here to celebrate and preserve. The party doesn't start till ten; when it ends, I don't remember. Back in the workaday world of the Northern Virginia suburbs, I would be asleep by now, instead of wondering why, uncomfortably clad in rutty tuxedo, I'm here at all.

Not just the party, but the Piedmont; not just me, but so many others as well. Why are we here? What is it about the Blue Ridge foothills that so fascinates and pulls people here? And why aren't those who would visit a theme park invited to join the fun?

To start with, visitors or newcomers would have had a hard time finding it — the PEC party, that is. There's no such thing as precise directions in a rural landscape whose inhabitants wish it to remain country. Until just a few months ago, you had to be a native or at least a long-time resident to have any notion of where you were going; for roads had names only orally, never fixed through signage, and postal addresses — like Rural Route 1, Box 350 — had no directional meaning. Now — to meet the requirements of 911 emergency service — any Tom, Dick, or Harry can find Bear Wallow Road or the Fodderstack, since the once mysterious names shine forth on bright new green-and-white street signs, as if the Piedmont has suddenly become suburbanized. This invasion of privacy, according to some oldtimers, will alter the Piedmont more than Disney ever would have. Still, there exists no road map to the most desirable locations, as a realtor might say. Such destinations remain tantalizingly vague — simply "The Oaks" is where this party is — but once you've been there, each of these grand residences with their commanding views remain forever fixed on the map of memory.

I had been this way before. No, not exactly — never before to The Oaks — but on a passage just like it, twisting and turning, following the contours of the land, a road designed for carriages not cars. Thirty some years ago. I was one of three teenagers in a used sportscar, newly bought with summer wages earned in sweaty hayfields, traveling too fast in late-night fog and drizzle. Rock-and-roll music bouncing off the stratosphere from a Buffalo, New York, station — that was our favorite — blared from the car radio, our only link to a world beyond the Piedmont. And what linked the rural counties of the Piedmont, tied them together, then as well as now, were roads and cars. When they're blocked, as in a recent June flooding, a neighborly sense of community is converted into a very rugged isolation.

"Living in the Piedmont means you're always 50 miles from somewhere," says a friend I've known since those days, Jay Adams, who still lives in northern Fauquier County and now works in Fredericksburg (yes, 50 miles away), where he runs the distillery that makes Virginia Gentleman bourbon.

So we thought nothing of driving however long it might take to wherever we'd heard there might be a good party — to places with names like The Oaks, or maybe Oak Hill, Oakwood, Happy Oaks, Chestnut Oaks, who knows? A party somewhere. Just another party, that was our highest ambition, made life worth living. That Labor Day weekend 35 years ago — better known here as Warrenton Horse Show weekend — my car flipped over on the country road's slick curve. I can still see my best friend's lacerated face, another friend's shattered jaw, and my own lost ear, sheared and flopping, like van Gogh's. Rushed to the nearest hospital, and who should be waiting but my father, a country doctor who happened to be on call. He sewed my ear back on.

Today my scar's hardly visible, but memories like this always stay raw. The car was totaled; we were lucky to have survived. Many other friends were killed in similar accidents. (I had only one friend killed when thrown from a horse.) A family that lived less than a mile from me lost both a son and a daughter, their only children, in separate auto crashes a year apart. Here in the Piedmont, it seemed that if a car didn't kill the young people, it drove them away. Few of the people I grew up with live here anymore. They got in their cars and left.

"We gotta get out of this place." We sang along with the popular song's lyrics whenever it came on the car radio. "Gotta get out of this place if it's the last thing we ever do...."

"I had to leave," says Larry Wilkes, who has remained my friend despite the damage my car did to his face. "Dueling scars," he bragged when he lived in Germany. Now we're so old, he says, the Commonwealth of Virginia should erect one of its Historical Markers on the site of our crash. And why did he have to leave the Piedmont?

"It's simple. It's called a job," he says. But it was more than that, I think; for I'm reminded of what a venerable lady once told me years ago when I was rhapsodizing about the Piedmont's rural lifestyle: "Oh, but don't live here, it saps young men of ambition." Now a Washington-area developer, Wilkes is close enough to come back home to visit. "The best of both worlds," he says.

That's what a lot of Washingtonians do: live and work in the city and suburbs and visit the Piedmont on weekends. In that sense, as a weekend place, the Piedmont already is a theme park, with or without Disney. And the theme is this: to live out the agrarian ideal about which Founding Father Thomas Jefferson rhapsodized. After all, when Jefferson was in the White House, he too was in effect a Piedmont weekender.

Just about a mile from where I crashed my car as a teenager is now the site of Great Meadows, the new home to the Virginia Gold Cup horse races. I say "new," because anything less than a quarter-century-old is new in the Piedmont. New, too, is Interstate 66. In no way a country road, it's the dagger, dripping suburbanized growth behind it, that strikes fear into the heart of the traditional Piedmont way of life. It's an uneasy truce of sorts that brings the two together — suburban and rural Virginia — every year on the first Saturday of May. That's the date for the annual running of the Virginia Gold Cup.

Cars spill off the interstate's The Plains/Middleburg exit, carrying more than 50,000 people to partake of the Piedmont for a glorious (if it's not raining) spring afternoon. Then they get in their cars and go back to where they came from. Not much different from what would have happened at Disney's America theme park, just a few miles away through Thoroughfare Gap — except, of course, the latter attraction would have enticed the public every day.

Also there's a certain hidden, save-the-Piedmont logic to the recent commercialization of an old Virginia, secret-society-like ritual such as the Gold Cup — with its ever growing crowds and purses, corporate sponsors like BMW, plus aggressive marketing and advertising that once would have been considered unseemly. The logic goes like this:

The more popular horse sports become, the better for the equestrian business; horse farms need open spaces; the Piedmont is thus preserved. In this scenario, simply driving west on Interstate 66 can help the cause: The passing farmland provides such an aesthetic experience that no one who has experienced it will ever want to see it developed.

Still, the new Gold Cup and the traffic it draws from the Washington metropolitan area are a bit much for some long-time race-goers: "I never go anymore. It's been ruined," they say. It's a Piedmont version of the uncertainty principle: the event itself has been altered by those observing it. "There're too many people, you can't even see the horses. But, of course, the people who are there don't care. They're too busy looking at each other."

Too many people, too little land. That's the fear in this place called Piedmont, that the name may stay the same but its way of life will be inevitably destroyed, as more and more people want a piece of the Piedmont. It's a land perhaps too beautiful for its own good. Here's Bob Dennis, former head of the Piedmont Environmental Council (PEC), explaining what makes the Piedmont different:

"The land's not cut up in little pieces. It's one of the few places left, like Vermont and the South Carolina and Georgia coast, with remnants of Jefferson's land ethic. It's a mix of well-tended, managed fields and still wild land. There're even been sightings of cougar. But don't say I saw a cougar; people wouldn't believe me, would think I'd been drinking!"

The influx of newcomers or "come-heres" — as opposed to "been-heres" — is evidenced on the rural road in Rappahannock County where Dennis lives. Only one tract of land — of several thousand acres — has remained whole, with continuous ownership in the same family, since the last century. "Everybody else living along Poe's Road has moved there since I've been there, within the last 40 years," says Dennis. What's wrong with that?

"In order to maintain traditions and the beauty of the landscape, a critical mass of farm land is needed. That means tracts no smaller than 100 acres." Such comments reveal an inegalitarian attitude, according to the PEC's pro-growth critics. But Dennis, neither a foxhunter nor a wealthy man, doesn't come across as an elitist, and many of what are often termed here the "five-acre people" would even agree with him. These newcomers don't want growth, either. They want a view out their living rooms windows of unspoiled landscape — not of other, newer five-acre people.

Or how about a view of a hog farmette? That's how a large local landowner fought one of the first subdivision developments that I can remember here, sometime in the late 1950s or early 1960s. As quickly as construction crews erected the single-family ramblers, he created the sloppiest, smelliest pig farm he could on his land right next to them. Needless to say, new home sales were less than brisk; but it was great fun for those of us already living here to get in our cars and drive out and watch the piglets wallow.

Since then, land-use battles have grown considerably more sophisticated if no less passionately intense, with the advent of complicated zoning ordinances, citizens groups like the PEC, and ever more lawyers. Land-use is the wedge issue here, cutting through party lines and statewide election campaigns; whether you voted for Chuck Robb or Ollie North is less important than how you feel about Walmart's coming. The clerk's office in each jurisdiction's county seat bustles as if it were Capitol Hill on otherwise laid-back Main Streets. Pass the Confederate monument, which stands vigil in front of every Virginia courthouse, flow the title examiners, surveyors, real estate attorneys, individual landowners and would-be landowners in search of deeds and plats to make at least part of the Piedmont theirs...or deny it from others. All this commotion has had its effect:

The Piedmont has probably changed more in my lifetime than in the two centuries after Alexander Spotswood and his Knights of the Golden Horseshoe first opened it to development. That's not just an egocentric statement by a typically boastful Baby-Boomer. But the Baby Boom most certainly had something to do with it, as did the postwar growth of the federal government. The populations of the Piedmont counties closest to Washington — Loudoun (about 90,000) and Fauquier (50,000) — have more than quadrupled and doubled, respectively, since 1950. For the first 50 years of the 20th Century their population had not grown at all.

Even the Piedmont counties to the west, with no such population growth, have changed in fundamental ways. Rappahannock County, for instance, actually lost population — from a high of almost 10,000 residents in 1850 to about 7,000 today — as former slave families migrated to the city and young people who, like my friend Wilkes, felt they had to leave. "Young out, retired in." That's the migration pattern, as described by one native, who adds, "It's gotten so people who actually work are becoming a smaller and smaller part of the population around here. Kind of like a country club. But when the people who left get enough money, they'll come back home. They'd kill if they have to."

Yes, there's something about the land here; it makes you do crazy things. I've already said that I once could have killed a man. Another irrational act — curiously even harder to admit — is that I lost a lot of money on the land here. If you saw it — in a Virginia version of "it seemed like a good idea at the time" — you'd understand: One of the most historic estates in the county, with unparalleled views of the Blue Ridge, it was almost bought by foreign money with questionable development plans. Instead, the buyers ended up being a local investment group of which I was a partner. We would not only make money — the price we paid was well below market — but preserve the estate as well. But this was 1989, the very top of the real estate boom. Like a lot of other people, we went bust.

The lesson I learned is this: You do not buy a Piedmont estate, no matter how beautiful or how historic, with borrowed money. The Piedmont may be a place for old money, even new money; but it's not a good home for debt. I remember walking the grounds of the grand estate and feeling weak from the interest payments that seemed to be sucked through my feet. To come up with cash, to try to make the land pay for itself, I suddenly found myself in the cattle business, despite the solicited, succinct advice of the Northern Virginia developer Til Hazel, justly renowned for his Midas Touch with anything to do with land: "Cows won't do it."

That brings me to something that might get me into even more trouble — not losing money, but losing friends. ("Are you sure you *really* want to write about the Piedmont?" warns my old buddy Wilkes.) Everybody knows it, but few here say it: It's an idle wealth that preserves the Piedmont. The people who own the grand country estates don't actually "do" anything; or, put another way, the wealth that maintains the land has absolutely nothing to do anymore with the land itself. In the Piedmont there no longer exists any direct relationship between land, labor, and wealth. The land no longer creates anything that society values sufficiently — is willing to pay for — to cover the cost of the land. The land is symbolic only, but certainly more enduring than a new Jaguar, more visible than stocks, bonds, and bank accounts. The wealth is there for all to see; it's real, this real estate, magically transforming the least likely candidates into overnight country squires. Here, farms become toys.

What would Jefferson say? Before you put words in his mouth — as it seems everybody here does to justify just about any position — remember that he himself was "land-poor" (too much land, not enough cash), almost bankrupt when he died. So, instead, listen to other Piedmont Virginians in the here and now:

"Real Virginians don't have money, if they ever did. They have cultivated the appearance of having money. That's better than money. No burdens," laughs a Piedmont native who has made and lost a fortune or two over the years buying and selling the land where he was born and raised.

"There are fundamentally three uses for land," allows Charlie Seilheimer, founder of Sotheby's International Realty, who moved from upstate New York to the Piedmont three decades ago. "The first is agricultural or other economic uses, like extracting minerals. Iowa rates a '10' in this regard, but who wants to live there? The second is for development purposes, but that's like spending your capital. finally, there is the value of ambience, of feeling. That's what the Piedmont offers. To come and live here is a gentlemanly pursuit."

A pursuit of happiness that's much too easy, according to another, newer newcomer: "People here don't have to work to pursue truth and beauty. They can just look out the window. There's too much money, too much alcohol, not enough to do. So idle, they even get bored by the beauty of the landscape."

"There are people like that everywhere, rich and poor alike," counters Seilheimer. "Wealth simply magnifies character flaws, the small made big, like the ancient gods. The same goes for the Piedmont's reputation for sex and murder scandals. Certainly, it's never boring here. How could they say that? I've been to dinner parties here where 10 of the 14 guests had been married to each other's partners. Men change women and horses often. That's sin and damnation in the view of Puritans like Roger Williams. But here in the Piedmont, it's more like metaphysical love poetry."

Virginia is for lovers — but not tattlers. What am I doing even asking such questions of people I know? It's like sitting in the front row of pews, which Episcopalians never do. Or being what the foxhunting crowd calls a "thruster," acting too socially aggressive, pushing to the head of the pack. Or needing a biographical dictionary to decipher the shorthand and code of those ubiquitous Virginia Historical Markers, which hardly ever use first names or identifying titles; it's just assumed you know who Jackson and Longstreet were. When explanations are not needed, inquiry is adolescently impolite.

"Did you come home to die?" my older daughter sometimes teases me. She can't understand why any sentient, still breathing being would forgo Inside-the-Beltway soap-opera for the sleepy pace of a Victorian novel in the Virginia Piedmont village where I grew up, which she and her 14-year-old sister have christened "Borrrrington."

My clichéd explanations don't satisfy her. Nor me. So I laugh, curiously reminded of that evangelist who threatened his flock that, unless they gave more money, "God will call me home."

Heaven right here on earth: That's certainly how the Piedmont is portrayed when threatened by those who, like a greedy Satan, would too much love God and the land He created: "They destroy what attracted them here in the first place," it is said of the newcomers whose contemporary homes subdivide the rolling countryside. And this of the aborted Disney America theme park: "It would have killed the very history it professed to celebrate." It was a holy war — that fight over the soil and soul of the Piedmont — "filled with religious significance," in the words of Piedmont resident, British transplant, and spy chronicler (*Treason in the Blood*) Anthony Cave Brown.

Even my daughters, who fondly remember trips to florida's Disney World, hated the notion of a theme park in the Piedmont. To them, who grew up in Alexandria, Arlington, and Fairfax, the Piedmont already is some kind of theme park, having very little to do with the real world as they know it — that is, the same suburban world of most younger Americans, squarely placed in the geography of nowhere. A sense of time and place is the Piedmont's theme. It's not a place to live a life (as in "get a life!"), but somewhere to go to visit grandparents and hear stories. If it didn't exist, it would be imagined. A pocket of make-believe in a world that is too much with us. In the end,

maybe that's the true value of any place called home— some imaginary place that never changes. Just the idea of it, that's enough. Anything more might be too much. To actually live there, then is it ruined?

I seek out my peers, people with whom I went to grade school, wanting to ask them. Why did they stay while others — indeed, most — left? But, of course, I never really ask. I wouldn't get a straight answer, anyway. Out here discussing personal affairs is just not done. It would be like trying to describe how beautiful a particular mountain view is. Instead, we talk about the weather.

But while getting my hair cut one day, I get my best answer yet — like (I smile at the simile) thinning the woods to get a better view. It's the same barber shop where four generations of my family have had their hair cut, including my curious daughter; though then a toddler, she no longer remembers. The recent high school graduate who's cutting my hair remarks that she has never seen me before; I say I grew up here and only recently moved back home.

"Oh, I would never leave. My family's here. It's so pretty here. I'm happy here," she says, snipping above my ears. "I guess you only leave if you're not happy."

So for me, now, is there happiness only in nostalgia? Is that why I'm here, returned home to a place that may exist only in memory? Is the purpose purely aesthetic, perhaps to partake the restful sunsets over the ever present Blue Ridge? Or is it just those simple, little indulgences like rich, extra-thick *real* milkshakes at the fountain in the corner drugstore that may soon go out of business? The 18th and 19th Century vernacular architecture that was meant not merely to please but to last? My front lawn's towering tulip poplar tree whose massive trunk takes three of us, arms extended, to embrace? The friendly waves from people you don't even know?

I can't answer my daughter's question. It doesn't matter, for this story's only about me insofar as self is shaped by place. The story's the Virginia Piedmont — and, its protectors would say, the Piedmont's story concerns us all.

"America was born on a farm in Virginia," solemnly and repeatedly intones the disembodied, God-like voice-over in the video developed by the Piedmont Environmental Council in its fight against Disney. The sentimentalized script often sounds like Cold War propaganda, and the production quality pretends to the glitziest Hollywood (even Disney) standards. But no one could quarrel or take issue with the visuals: The Piedmont *is* beautiful, picture perfect. And it's true: In the beginning was the word, specifically the words of the Declaration of Independence and the Federalist Papers, spilling from the brains of Jefferson and Madison, whose bodies were grounded in the Virginia Piedmont. Also true: On this ground were fought some of the bloodiest battles of the Civil War, forging a more perfect Union. So it is that, in daring to put the Piedmont into words, I must come to this conclusion:

The Piedmont is not merely my home — but that of all Americans, even unappreciative teenagers. If not literally where they were born and reared, then it is the home of their ancestors. If not their genealogical forbears, then at least their founding fathers. And these progenitors, too, felt at home here, the receptively fertile soil for their ideas to do nothing less than to create a new country; it could be everything their original homeland was and wasn't — nostalgia blended with an enlightened England of their own invention. So the Piedmont's landscape must be in our blood. Its gentrified good life is what dreams are made of. To make them real, to ground them in the land, we'd even fight. ❧

Sunday Drives and the Meaning of Life

A personal essay is like a Sunday drive. This occurs to me while, yes, on a Sunday drive. Going nowhere in particular, with neither a map, as in a carefully plotted novel, nor a fixed destination, as in a well reasoned dissertation.

Stopping here and there: For a cup of coffee at a country store, crowded with other, nodding coffee-drinkers as if it were communion. To lean over the rail midway on a one-lane bridge for a closer look below at a familiar river, usually quiet and so small it should be called a stream, suddenly turgid from a heavy thunderstorm upstream. To pause and consider the massive Sycamore ripped from the riverbank, with such a skeletal, intricately webbed root system now exposed to air and light and rushing water and so soon to be picked clean of its red flesh of earthly clay. A passing glimpse of a turn-of-the-last century, dilapidated barn, sorely in need of roof and siding to cover once load-bearing, now purposeless, posts and beams with their handhewn notches, naked, for all the world to see if only anyone would take a moment, a fraction of the time it took to make them. To pull off the road to read an historical marker, where "from this spot two miles south and one-half mile west...."

Or sometimes not stopping at all....

Just to keep moving is the point if there is one — even if it means simply poking along, driven by (and free to play out) inward-looking, meandering thoughts, leading who knows where? To share, if you're lucky, with a traveling companion, whatever these notions are that you'd normally have only alone. To go exploring, as I used to tell my children. To go antiquing, as my mother would tell her only child and so fashion a practical and domestic veneer (finding that perfect piece of furniture) around her own true reason — to instill a sense of appreciation for the world into which she'd brought him, a never dying curiosity about what's around the road's next bend. To mix the joy of discovery — as if he were the very first to see this place on earth — with the comfort of belonging. No, he really wasn't the first, but he could share the emotion of those from "the olden days" (his mother's phrasing) who had come before him.

Then, the rhythm changes, quickens. Who cares that speed limits or other rules and structures like literary conventions are broken in the hurry to get there, somewhere even if it's nowhere, wherever it is that these thoughts are leading?

You can't get there from here. Those words of futility we've all heard before. Sometimes they come from within (as in writer's block). More often, they're warnings from others — spoken not always aloud (more often with just a look) by people like the wizened, not necessarily wise, old men rocking on the creaky porch of the crossroads store. They often simply smile and stare should the Sunday driver be foolish enough to ask directions.

Maybe I can't get there, but I'll try at least and see what happens, laughs the essayist. That, after all, is the essay's

essence — to try, to make an effort, to test. I'll take a right at the next fork just to see where it goes. Exploring the landscape of the possible, the world of wonder and whimsy, is what it's all about, is where fun is found. Making connections where there was none. They can happen on a hunch — turning right instead of left — and nothing more.

And sure enough, I always end up back where I started from. Home. All roads lead there, eventually. Everything is connected, ultimately. That's the very definition of a Sunday drive: to be back home by the end of the day. To go so many miles, to spend all these words — a reasonable person might ask — only to go nowhere?

That's life.

In search of God and meaning, a travel essayist might grandly broadcast his intentions by making a trip, say, to Nepal. With round-trip ticket in hand, however, the final destination still remains the same — home. Approaching the seemingly simple, familiar concept of home from another, foreign angle produces the best of travelers' epiphanies, even the most exotic. (For that matter, the work of just about any expatriate author usually ends up angling back home.)

Like church-going, the tradition of Sunday drives teaches the truth of the circular nature of things, another expression of which is ritual. There's no such thing as linear movement in the rolling Piedmont, whose largely agricultural landscape is still cyclically tied to the seasons.

The shortest distance between two points has little meaning here. To forsake the false God of the new and different — what's news, what's hot, whether Sunday morning television's noisemaker interviews or the weekend sales at Northern Virginia's many suburban malls — is the essence of the old-fashioned Sunday drive.

Except for clearly defined goals — to watch the autumn leaves turn, to visit a distant relative, and, yes, to go mall-hopping for best bargains — few people go on Sunday drives anymore. Fewer still read, much less write, essays. What does that say about their value, the worth of what I'm doing? Certainly, there's little money in it; yet is the activity priceless because so rare? Such questions, of course, are not original and go to the heart of what's good, whether the good is necessarily synonymous with the popular.

The good, the best people, it is said, no longer answer the call of public service. Where, it is asked, are the Jeffersons, the Madisons (those Piedmont men) when we need them? They are unwilling to submit themselves to popularity contests, to have their private lives made public with information the people crave. Celebrities are another story.

The whole world is watching. The whole world is watching. The whole world is watching.... Watching me, that's who the world was watching. Yes, I was there. You probably were, too — if not physically there, you were watching on TV. There's where the whole world was watching, on television — the 1968 Chicago Convention. The chant arose everywhere around me — on the streets, the parks, and the convention floor — as I was there, too, a young journalist who sympathized with the protesters. A participant-observer is what people like me called ourselves then. In my dingy white, beat-up Volkswagen bug, I had traveled non-stop from rural Virginia just to be in Chicago that August. I would make a difference. If I couldn't be in Czechoslovakia to witness and participate in the final days of the "Prague spring" that August, I would be in Chicago.

I am reminded of that time because, as I write this, now 28 years later, another Democratic Convention is being held in Chicago, the first since 1968. I am not there, and I'm not watching. Why? Would the answer be a commentary on the public arena or introspective analysis of the older, presumably wiser, me?

To make sense of experience, what it is exactly to live a life, that's what one thinks about on a Sunday drive — not while dashing to a plane to make the next political rally, business meeting, or rendezvous with destiny. As our lives are measured not in teaspoons but with a diet of daily, fast-breaking events against the grand sweep of history, the days pile up like old newspapers saved to be reread, and I find myself wondering less and less about what happens next — and, instead, simply trying to piece together the jagged edges of a puzzle neither cleanly nor clearly cut.

So it is that I am drawn to the literary essay. It is an

inviting road, in the old, almost lost tradition of belles lettres, where the writing is an end in itself, necessarily neither practical nor informative. So-called "news you can use," an essay is not. Rather, it reflects an acute self-consciousness of what came before and what lies ahead — like the road traveled by a Sunday driver. The essayist's ambition, no more, no less, is an "awareness of indebtedness to history, scholarship, literature, the acutest nuances of language." Those are the words of Cynthia Ozick in her own essay "It Takes a Great Deal of History to Produce a Little Literature," whose title is indebted to the words of someone else — the novelist Henry James.

My awareness is of time and place. My indebtedness is to the Piedmont of Virginia.

In itself, a Sunday drive doesn't mean much, doesn't much matter. Certainly, it'll never make headlines like a good soundbite on the Sunday morning newsmaker interview that you missed. No history will be written about Sunday drives, what happened when, no what-if scenarios about the road not taken. But I bet the beginnings of a historian's enlightening narrative flow might well be written *during* Sunday drives. Because if you don't kick up too much dust, you can see for miles. It can even lead you to meaning.

But a Sunday drive on a dusty road today is the equivalent of too much information in this Age of Information. There are too many thoughts that need to be sorted; a good rain is needed to wet them down with clarity. To see the world as a child again, not confused by clouds of dust and shades of gray. Either it's raining or it's not raining; such tautological truths are all we can know with any certainty, said Wittgenstein, whose work once so enthralled me that I traveled to Vienna to study under his disciples. Much older now, I wonder whether it might be even simpler than either/or.

For when we're born, the world is one, we'd probably say if we could talk. Childhood development and learning is all about making distinctions — mama and papa, self and other, black and white, life and death — and finding the words to delineate the differences. The finer the lines, the better, and supposedly the more educated and knowledgeable we become. So it's said.

An old man becomes a child again, it's also said. Before I die, I hope to become an old man. An old man, his old wife by his side, on a Sunday drive. Knowing that what is seen and thought is inevitably altered by memories of observations and thoughts from the last trip, and the ones before that, layered in time. Knowing that when I die, they'll die, too, for they live only in the consciousness of them. Thus the urge to write? To write, to make connections, to tie everything together, to make all one again. That is, to come home again. Home, for me, to the Virginia ❦

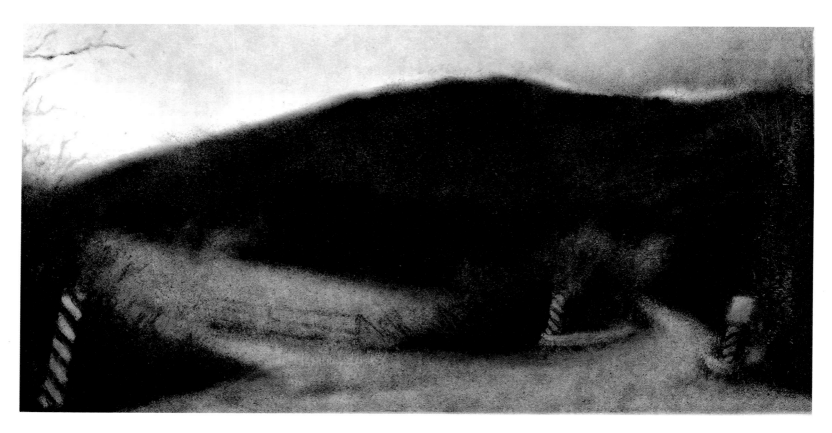

The Mountains Whose Name Is Gone

TODAY, as many as 8,000 years later, in freshly turned cornfields on the floodplains of the Rivanna, Rapidan, and Rappahannock you can still find what they made — so finely crafted, so indestructible, so timeless, as if actually made for you, for you to discover, and then for you to leave for others, yet unborn, to find anew. They seem almost alive — these quartzite and basalt spear points or arrowheads — though they were made to kill.

By the time the first English explorers pushed up the Chesapeake estuaries, the Indians who inhabited these banks were the Algonquin tribes of the Powhatan Confederacy, including the Pamunkey, the Mattaponi, the Chickahominy, the Nansemond, and the Rappahannock. These tribal designations all still live, attached now to Virginia tidal rivers of the same names.

Upstream, above the fall line, were other Indians about which less is known. By the time European settlers encountered and described them, disease and dislocation had altered their Precontact ways. Nomadic, they tended to make their home along the rivers and streams while hunting buffalo and other game. These upland Indians of the Piedmont included the Tanxnitania and Whokentia tribes of the Manahoac (Algonquin for "they were very merry"), who were often warred upon from the north by the Iroquois, whose trail crossed the Rappahannock at Norman's Ford. Like the Manahoac, other Siouan-speaking groupings apparently inhabited the Piedmont, too —

the Saponi, Tutelo, Occaneechi, and Monacan.

But very little, not even the name, is known of those who came before — now called by students of America's prehistory simply as "Formative" or "Woodland" cultures. Evidence of the state's only known "cliff kill" site — where the earliest Indians would drive game over the edge of a sheer drop — has been discovered in the Shenandoah National Park near the Rapidan River's Blue Ridge headwaters.

Downstream in the more densely populated Tidewater, the approximately 6,000-square-mile chiefdom of the Powhatan's 32 tribes is estimated to have numbered about 9,000 — living in as many as 200 separate villages. Unlike the less cohesive Iroquois to the north, the Powhatan were organized as true tribes (or bands) in a confederacy; and the ruler had absolute power, even over life and death. Also unlike many other Native Americans, a vague concept of private property apparently existed, whereby individuals and kinship groups "owned" land, its hunting rights and fishing sites.

The Powhatans wore hides, furs, and materials made out of plants. Their moccasins were soft, with a continuous sole. Their dwellings, which two or more families shared, were generally rectangular, with barrel-shaped roofs, sometimes called "long houses." While men built the houses and hunted and gathered, the women cultivated maize and other crops, including tobacco. They crafted pottery, and their woven baskets were plaited.

Their language, spoken, not written, is believed to have been a variation of that of the Delaware Indians, also Algonquins. Powhatan priests were responsible for places of worship and burial. The Powhatans held various beliefs about an afterlife and called their primary anthropomorphic god "okeus."

As the Indians were gradually pushed upstream by the colonists, records show that in 1669 two villages of the Portobago tribe near Occupacia Creek numbered "60 bowmen and hunters" and that in 1684 what remained of the Rappahannock tribe, near Tappahannock, were transported 35 miles upstream. The last known village in the Rappahannock watershed was at a place called Indiantown on the Rapidan. Near the Lands End Wildlife Management Area in King George County, on the Rapphannock's Nanzatico Bay, is an archeological site of what in the late 1600s was the largest Indian village on the river — now designated a Virginia Historic Landmark.

South of the tidal Rappahannock, in King William County, are now two Indian Reservations for the Mattaponi and the Pamunkey — all that remains of the Powhatan domain. As for the Piedmont Indians, only a few Monacan descendants survive. Recognized by the Virginia General Assembly as one of eight formally organized tribal governments, they live on or near Bear Mountain in Amherst County. Their language is English.

To recount all this, as I have just done, makes me sad. And to have done it so matter-of-factly, even sadder. So why did I feel compelled to do it all, to set down in my own written language the little that I know of the Indians, my spatial ancestors, who once lived where I do now? Scholars, of course, know more than I; indeed, much of what I, a layman, think I know may well be wrong; so it is with some risk that I have even tried to put figurative pen to paper.

That I know so little, maybe that's what makes me sad.

At night, sometimes, I go outside and stare at the stars. My eyes are pulled downward toward the Blue Ridge Mountains. They are darker even than the night. I find my mind wondering, imagining how an Indian, my predecessor, looked at these mountains, what he saw, what he thought, what he felt, what they meant to him. And, most of all, I wonder what was the name he called them, these dark mountains to the west that swallow the sun, by what name was suggested their mysterious presence and power?

To die, to have your children die, and their childless children die, your gods die, your genes extinguished, your race eradicated, never to be remembered, that is death enough. But to leave ignorance not only for your own name but also for the names that you gave to the places you loved — that must be oblivion. ❧

Love, Betrayal, and the Rappahannock

THIS is a ghost story. A tale of childhood, of innocence and paradise lost. It is also, like all stories emanating from nearby Washington, D.C., a parable of power, decisions, second-guessing, and compromised values as the very private and personal is made oh, so public. But most of all, it is a story of love and betrayal; and so I should begin with this confession: I've never been totally faithful. I always flirt with others. Whenever I leave Northern Virginia's Piedmont, I test the waters.

The Penobscot, Snake, Cowpasture, Nantahala, Brandywine, and the Potomac watershed's Cacapon and Shenandoah: I cherish their names and their rich connotations. Others seduce me: the Mississippi and Missouri headwaters, the Colorado, and the Hudson (upstate, of course). Faraway Scottish lochs, England's tiny Ouse, and some uncommonly pristine freshets in the hills around Vienna and Prague whose identities were quickly lost and forgotten as they rushed toward the meandering, mighty Danube. I've canoed, kayaked, rafted or been baptized by—fallen into, leapt into, and sometimes seriously swum—them all. But I keep coming home to Northern Virginia, and its Rappahannock River. Like Northern Virginia itself—the now Yankee-like region of an otherwise still Southern, largely agrarian state, whose suburban and high-tech growth was driven by the funny money of Washington unreality—the river has ambiguous qualities. Long, monotonous, flat stretches are interspersed with some of the most exciting whitewater in the Chesapeake basin—the rapids at Kelly's Ford, Snake Castle, the Rapidan confluence, and the Fredericksburg fall line— as the river drains the eastern slope of the Blue Ridge. Named by the Indians for its rapidly rising and falling waters, the Rappahannock can slow to a trickle in the summer yet immediately swell to a muddy-colored flood after heavy thunderstorms.

Although smack in the midst of the Eastern Seaboard's urban corridor, the 185-mile-long Rappahannock has withstood most development pressures. There is little pollution besides some agricultural and small-town runoff. And, except for Fredericksburg's water-supply containment dam, the river remains free-flowing despite intense past attacks from the Army Corps of Engineers. Between the few bridges that cross the river, the landscape the Rappahannock traverses is still so wild that a British canoeing companion once told me it brought back subtropical memories of his boyhood in Rhodesia, now Zimbabwe.

Whatever the often fuzzy appellation "Northern Virginia" really means, the Rappahannock helps define it. The river offers the region a clear southern and western boundary. Together with the Potomac to the east and north, the Rappahannock carves Virginia's Tidewater into the land called the Northern Neck, which, extended westward into the Piedmont and the mountains, was once the land-granted property of Lord Fairfax.

But can anyone own the river? Certainly the Rappahannock owns my childhood and its summer memories. Remembrance may be clouded, I admit, for the sun never seemed bright in one spot; rather, its white heat was diffused evenly in the humid haze, just as the buzz of insects was everywhere in the canopy of chestnut oaks, tulip poplars, and cottonwoods. But I know the river was always clear, even when the skies were not, and cool when the air was steamy. The sweet and sticky honeysuckle scents; the slippery, red-clay banks punctuated by sharp, rocky outcroppings that geologists say were once part of what is now Africa; the ubiquitous thick-green foliage— all meant that the world was endlessly full of promise and possibility, which my friends and I were put on this earth to discover and to explore. And by discovering and exploring, we would thereby conquer and possess— ourselves maybe, but the river never.

Captain John Smith was our hero, and it was easy to imagine that we were he, now encountering these same, ever changing waters for the first time. There was little room in our new world for the complications of a Pocahontas, from whom our hero was "saved" by his friend John Rolfe's marriage. Nor did we care to understand the complications of commerce—the hard, grown-up business of competitively yet cooperatively dealing with peoples other than ourselves, whose dominion over the land that the river drained seemed embodied by Pocahontas's fierce father, Chief Powhatan.

Now my two daughters are young as I was then. Their school ends and summer begins with our annual rite of passage down the Rappahannock. We put our canoe in as far upstream, near the source at Chester's Gap, as the spring rains allow. The river is so narrow here that a single fallen tree or a cattle farmer's possessive fence necessitates a portage. Such obstacles form part of the adventure; we are going exploring.

Each bend in the old river brings something new; if we are quiet, even surprises: whitetails bending to drink from its waters, turtles sunning on a rock, a snake entwined in an overhanging branch, a duck fluttering vulnerably to distract us from her offspring. Had it not been for the Rappahannock, my own children might not be here now. They were born from a love for a woman whose family lived downstream at the mouth of the Rappahannock, where it enters the Chesapeake. Fate needn't lie in the stars but in currents right here on earth. As the children became toddlers, they would float messages in bottles down the river toward their grandparents. It was an exploration into the forces of nature—gravity, displacement—and of love. Now, as evening falls over our sycamore-embowered campsite on a midstream sandbar or in a daisy of a meadow right at river's edge, ghosts become liminal. Yes, ghosts: Amid the murmuring ripples, pulsing frogs and singing katydids, you can discern the soft breathing of sleeping soldiers, blue and gray, tens of thousands of them. In the still-hot evening breeze, you can feel the presence

of these fathers—if not their actual bodies, the stories they told. I repeat them, the stories they told. Stories of that apparition in his own time, John Singleton Mosby, "The Gray Ghost" who used the landscape carved by the river's upstream tributaries to elude the Northern intruders. Of the young artillery officer whom Robert E. Lee called "my gallant Pelham," killed at Kelly's Ford. And stories, of course, of Stonewall Jackson, mistakenly shot from his horse by his very own men among the dense spring foliage and underbrush near the river at Chancellorsville, felled at the precise moment of his greatest victory. For this was the bloody Rappahannock line that divided Lee's Army of Northern Virginia and the multi-headed Army of the Potomac, the line that served to separate Richmond and Washington. In some senses, it was an artificial line—the rolling Piedmont estates north of the river were just as "Southern" as Lowcountry plantations. Yet the natural barrier of the Rappahannock, forcing armies to ford and flank, was as real as a fault line running through the heart of the nation. Onto the campfire you throw another piece of driftwood. Still damp, it wheezes, and you hear steel teeth on bone. Before he died, Jackson's left arm, shattered by the furious fusillade, was amputated, you remember, and you cannot sleep. There are other ghosts. Your own. Lost youth can become a demon. The betrayal is as unintentional as the shots that mortally wounded Jackson—and just as deadly. That my professional life became devoted to words, and (as a publisher) finding the money to print them, can be traced to the Rappahannock. The very first story I ever wrote was about whitewater canoeing. It was published in *Boy's Life*. I was 13, the same age as my younger daughter, now sleeping by the campfire on the river. I could be she. Or she I, a third of a century ago.

And when she is my age now? I'll no doubt be a ghost…if I'm lucky. Will I haunt the Rappahannock? Will it have me? Will there even be a Rappahannock? I wonder.   For unlike ghosts, people and their populations use water as they use money. It circulates, it gets wasted, it slips through our fingers. So too does the Rappahannock become simply and ultimately mere water.

In 1986, I started and published a magazine devoted to Northern Virginia called *New Dominion*. Its pages chronicled the "go-go" commercial and residential development that became synonymous with the region and that even began to lap the banks of the Rappahannock. I did more, I confess, than report on Northern Virginia's perhaps inevitable growth; the magazine was driven by it. Real estate advertisements paid the bills; without them, there would have been no magazine.

So it was one day—a day like any other in the publishing business, when meeting a press deadline had become the sole purpose of my personal history—that one particular full-page, four-color ad caught my attention. Its beautiful photographic images captured the Rappahannock landscape of my youth—now for sale, carved into site plans for high-density development.

It was a stretch of the river I knew well, my first and favorite campsite. I remember that very first overnight trip: the uneasy sleep after swapping ghost stories with my tentmate, then being frightened awake by the thud of something on the canvas. Only when we dared to stick our heads out of the flaps did we see scattered pine cones, hurled by our laughing parents come to check up on us. It was the very spot where, later, I had tried out my hand-made foldboat, built a rope bridge, fished for bass, gigged for frogs, and swung Tarzan-like from the tree limbs to splash in the best swimming hole around.

The development now planned for this spot I also knew very well, from its conservationist opponents, my friends. They had pointed out that in dry months, when the upper Rappahannock shrivels to little more than a creek, the development's projected waste water discharge would actually exceed, in gallons per day, the river's flow. Treated waste, true, but still waste. Lots of it. Should I pull the ad? I asked myself.

As with any such conflict of wills and wants, the issue, though perhaps irrelevant in the larger Washington policy-wonk scheme of things, was complicated. There were questions of private conscience and public morality, of ethics and good business practices, even of first Amendment rights. And less lofty questions as well: The ad dollars were going to be spent regardless; why shouldn't my magazine take its share? And no matter that the magazine's advertising contracts clearly gave me the discretion to reject ads: Could I legitimately let my personal feelings penalize my publishing company's investors and employees? I had, of course, bills to pay, a payroll to meet. The magazine wasn't just a personal toy; a business never is. Even the boss is always accountable to others—whether shareholders, future generations, or ghosts.

I never shared my private doubts; the issues were never discussed; for running a business is like running the rapids. You get swept up in the current. Decisions are instantaneous. To second-guess yourself means you capsize. The presses ran. I did my job.

I did my job — isn't that what compromised people always say, even what mid-level Nazis rationalized? But am I not being silly, pretentious even, to worry still that what I did or didn't do had consequences that were grand?

You don't have to be a connoisseur of ironic incongruity to appreciate that the magazine never received payment for the ad, the development hasn't yet really gotten off the ground, the original developer's ad agency seems to have disappeared, and *New Dominion* magazine is no longer being published — all swamped by changing economic currents.

But, for now, the Rappahannock remains beautifully the same, as always. Did my decision ultimately matter? Only to me. ❧

Of Two Minds
Is the Piedmont

Of all the man-made creations on this earth, the United States is the one nation conceived in words — specifically, the Declaration of Independence and the Constitution. Other modern nation-states, those 19th-Century constructs, owe their existence essentially to dynastic and/or ethnic origins. But what's the origin of the words that created our country; where were they grounded; whence came the thoughts from which they sprung? The short answer, of course, is that they came from two minds of men from the Piedmont, Thomas Jefferson and James Madison — one as the author of the Declaration, the other as the traditionally called "Father of the Constitution." This leads to a longer, more complicated question, one over which I've puzzled and pondered for years; let me now pose it this way:

These two documents — the Declaration of Independence and the Constitution of the United States — are as different, yet as necessary to one another, as day and night. One is a call to revolution; the other, a counter-revolutionary framework for order. But the land that formed the lives of the two creators of these different documents — like the times and the books that shaped the thoughts of these generally like-minded individuals — was identical. One's immediate reaction must surely be, what a fertile ground is the Virginia Piedmont! But then, on reflection, one must wonder: How can the same landscape produce such equally powerful yet so disparate texts, reflecting such dissimilar ways of looking at the world? It's almost as if

Madison and Jefferson lived on separate planets, rather than less than a day's horseback or carriage ride apart.

Individuals are inherently good and infinitely perfectible, proclaims the Declaration. No, you must assume the very worst about human nature and behavior, counters the Constitution. The Declaration is premised on the rule of reason and a belief that people are ultimately rational and therefore wise, while the Constitution takes for granted the primacy and determinism of self-interest, and its sometimes irrational passions. The Declaration promulgates the natural rights of man, the foremost of which is freedom. But absolute freedom, without checks or balances, will lead inevitably to anarchy or, paradoxically, a new tyranny — and therein lies the necessity for Constitutional law.

Simply put, the Declaration is a work of soaring idealism, while realism, prudence, and pragmatism — if not downright pessimism — pervades every Constitutional clause. Even the Constitution's accompanying Bill of Rights doesn't speak of these rights and liberties in any kind of positive or uplifting way; rather, they are expressed in the negative as guarantees against oppression — worst-case scenarios are assumed a priori. And *The Federalist Papers*, illuminating the political theory behind the Constitution, are self-evidently the work of practical, not idealistic, men — Madison the Virginian together with New Yorkers Alexander Hamilton and John Jay, in real agreement, despite their regional and other differences, on the necessity for a strong national government.

It's as if philosophically and politically Jefferson viewed the world through rose-colored glasses and Madison preferred dark-tinted shades, while physically what they saw must have been exactly the same. The views from Jefferson's Monticello and Madison's Montpelier, their cherished homeplaces just 30 miles apart, were similar and largely remain today as they were then — cultivated and pastured hills softly rolling westward toward the mountains. Being situated on what locals sometimes call "the morning side of the Blue Ridge," Monticello and Montpelier should theoretically both lend themselves to metaphorical sunrises — optimism and its natural corollary, idealism. Likewise, the soil — a rich, red clay and loam, in contrast to the exhausted, thinly covered, sandy land of previous generations' low-lying Tidewater plantations. Though farming is always a challenge, there was nothing unusually adversarial in either man's relationship with nature or his neighboring landowners. And there was nothing unpleasant, much less mind-altering, in the water, as the land around Monticello and Montpelier are drained by generally peaceful, clean, and slow-moving rivers, the Rivanna and the Rapidan. Flowing toward their nearby confluences with the James and the Rappahannock, respectively, the Rivanna and the Rapidan are part of the same Chesapeake Bay watershed; there is no Continental Divide between them.

Both men were possessive of their tracts of land, from which they derived no small measure of their unique identities as individuals. A Jefferson without his Monticello is unimaginable. A disinherited Madison without his family's 4,000 productive acres on the banks of the Rapidan would not have had the financial independence that he considered necessary for honorable public service. On a personal level, the land lured both men into speculative investments involving still more real estate. On the level of the personal writ large — so-called national character — they had only to gaze westward at the massive silhouette of the Blue Ridge to envision the destiny and greatness of the American Frontier. Without their personally felt, firmly grounded understanding of the land, of its potential wealth, and of all the other endless possibilities it presented, the Louisiana Purchase — when Jefferson was President and Madison, his Secretary of State — would not have happened.

That they had the patented privilege to possess the enormous landholdings represented by Monticello and Montpelier went unquestioned. For the notion of private property rights, particularly as expressed by the English philosopher John Locke, provided the foundation for much of both men's personal values as well as their political theorizing. Indeed, in Jefferson's view, the pursuit of happiness was in many ways synonymous with the right to own land. In order to do away with poverty and inequality, Jefferson sounded like a 20th-Century developer when he once told legislators that they could not "invent too many devices for subdividing land." That home ownership would become the most common expression of the American Dream is not surprising.

The primary purpose of government was the protection of property, according to Madison, who defined property not simply as land or other possessions but also in "its larger and juster meaning [of everything] to which a man may attach a value or have a right." So, for Madison, property rights and human rights were equivalent. "In a word," he wrote, "as a man is said to have a right to his property, he may be equally said to have a property in his rights."

The deep, not always spoken, fear of any landowner is that his property might somehow be unjustly taken away. Certainly, this was in the back of the minds of the delegates to the Constitutional Convention when they debated the questions of suffrage and enfranchisement: Could the new Republic's irresponsible and envious rabble be trusted to respect the property rights of the landed classes? While there was general agreement on the Lockean principle that any government should exist only with the consent of the governed, there was considerable concern about who exactly would be conferring this "consent." That is, should nonfreeholders — those who owned no land — be allowed to vote? Despite his own selfish interest as part of the landowning class, Madison resisted fellow delegates's efforts to exclude the landless.

Instead, Madison put his faith in the universal right to acquire land through lawful means. Such a right would help make everyone a responsible stakeholder in the success of the new nation. Seen in this historical context, today's special-interest subsidies for the real estate industry, like mortgage-interest tax deductions, may be nobler than they appear.

For Jefferson and Madison, those enlightened Piedmont gentry, their interest in the land they owned was more than financial — and as natural as the rights they espoused. For Jefferson, this interest reflected an intellectual curiosity about the world around him that can only be called passionate. Politics, he frequently complained, was a detestable duty, a demanding distraction from his true pursuits of natural history and the physical sciences. Throughout his life he meticulously recorded observations on everything from the climate and horticulture to geology, zoology, and botany; here, for example, are the first entries in his *Garden Book*, begun in 1766: "March 30: Purple hyacinth begins to bloom. April 6: Narcissus and puckoon open. April 13: Puckoon flowers fallen. April 16: A bluish-colored funnel-formed flower in lower grounds in bloom."

The hungry eyes that so observed with such loving detail the unfolding Piedmont spring — and the mind that then felt compelled to record what was seen — do not jibe with today's image of a politician, conversant only in circumlocution. Nor do they belong to what we would call a very practical man, interested only in the utilitarian nature of things. Instead, the words read like poetry, with the subtly changing Piedmont seasons as Jefferson's muse. If it wasn't the land that made Jefferson a poet, at least it seems to have helped bring to the surface the sensitive side of an extremely complex, multifaceted personality, who matter-of-factly interspersed in the same *Garden Book* notes about plantings and yields of peas and carrots and cucumbers, as any good husbandman would.

No one would ever accuse Madison of having been a poet, but, like his friend and neighbor, he clearly had a deep attachment for the land on which he lived and prospered. As a young man, by all accounts, Madison had been a somewhat reluctant agrarian, having toyed with vocational and financial plans to escape the bonds of the family farm. With age, scientific studies, and experience, however, Madison grew to possess the greatest agricultural knowledge of any man in the world, according to Jefferson. Upon retirement from public life, Madison was chosen by neighboring farmers to be president of the Agricultural Society of Albemarle, whose practical mission was to bring scientific problem-solving and efficiencies to farming. Its larger, tacit mission was to help ensure the viability of agriculture in the new Republic, whose virtue and success, both Madison and Jefferson believed, was premised on the citizenry's fundamental agrarian character.

"Our red clay hills," is how Madison described the rich

farmland of the Piedmont during an 1818 address to the Society. These hills, he said, are ideal for planting maize and for contour plowing. With the application of corn stalks, various forms of animal manure, and chemical fertilizers, he counseled, exhausted fields could be rejuvenated. He then went on to talk about irrigation, the relative merits of oxen and horses for farm work, and a cost-benefit analysis of the milk, manure, and hides produced by thin or fat cows. Mathematical reasoning also revealed the need for restoring and conserving Virginia's depleted forests, Madison continued, as he explained precisely why each and every fireplace on a Piedmont farm required 10 acres of trees to provide sustainable, renewable fuel.

Giving voice so to what we today would call an environmental ethic seems precocious on Madison's part, if not anachronistic. Certainly, neither Madison nor Jefferson would have called themselves environmentalists, although they would have well understood what that designation would come to signify. For their rural roots in the Piedmont combined with the Enlightened Age in which they lived — a singular position in time and space — meant for them that reason and nature could coexist in harmonious and virtuous ways. Indeed, the future of the new Republic depended upon wise use of the country's uniquely endowed land.

Celebrating the land and its bounty was, for Jefferson, a patriotic act. "What a field we have at our doors to signalize ourselves," he wrote. Although his *Notes on the State of Virginia* was the result of painstaking research, objectively recorded, Jefferson often could not disguise his pride in, even awe at, the seemingly sublime perfection of his native land. The mountains that border the Piedmont, for example, "are not scattered confusedly over the face of the country" was the way he put it. "They commence at about one hundred and fifty miles from the sea coast, are disposed in ridges one behind the other running nearly parallel with the seacoast."

These Blue Ridge Mountains on the distant horizon dominate the vista from the portico at Montpelier, which, like most manor houses of the period, is situated on low-lying land near a river. By contrast, Monticello, as the Italian name implies, is set atop a "Little Mountain" — expanding the horizons, creating a panorama of 360 degrees. Montpelier looks out from the landscape of which it is a part. Monticello looks down; the prospect is of distance only. Given Jefferson's wide reading and naturalist interests, he might well have been familiar with these apt, Elizabethan lines from John Webster's *Duchess of Malfi*:

Glories, like glow-worms, afar off shine bright,
But look'd too near have neither heat nor light.

Besides its mountaintop site, Monticello was also unusual for its circular and octagonal designs, aesthetically pleasing but not necessarily practical for everyday living.

Square and rectangular shapes were customary for both exteriors and interior rooms in the Virginia architecture of the day, modeled after English residential dwellings and public buildings. But Italy provided far better architectural models, Jefferson hypothesized, since the Italian Piedmont's landscape and climate were so similar to the like-named Virginia region that was his home. And thus classic Italian forms, including Palladian windows and pillared porticoes, provided the architectural inspiration for Jefferson's new home on the 600-foot mountain rising above the 2,650 acres along the Rivanna that he had inherited from his father. Jefferson was 25 years old when construction began, and he would spend the next 40 years, as he phrased it, "putting up and tearing down."

Madison did not have to build his home; he inherited that, too, along with the surrounding farm acreage acquired by his grandparents in 1723. The plantation was named Montpelier after a royal estate in England. The earliest part of the manor house itself was built by Madison's father in 1755, and typically for such a house, wings and additions were added over the subsequent years. Most notably, in 1798 and in 1812, Madison employed two of Jefferson's own master builders to add a portico and to expand the house, as it stretched into a 55-room mansion.

The house was big, but the man was little — or, rather, as Aaron Burr put it, "a great little man." Madison stood only five feet, four inches tall, and weighed about one hundred pounds. "No bigger than half a piece of soap... a withered little apple-John," is the way the writer Washington Irving described "Jeemy" Madison. Since an apple-John was an apple considered to be perfect and ripe only when shriveled, the description may have been cruel but nonetheless warranted — given not only Madison's slight physique but also his quiet, barely audible voice and often frail health. Moreover, many historians have induced, Madison was infertile.

In contrast stood Jefferson. His body was tall, rangy, and energetic; his vigorous and sensual approach to the physical world was such that Alexander Hamilton even called Jefferson a "concealed voluptuary...in the plain garb of Quaker simplicity." Because of the unusually tall physical stature not only of Jefferson but also of George Washington, George Mason, the Randolphs, and the Lees, "it was for a long time believed in England that the Virginians approached the gigantic," according to a chronicler at the time. "Madison was probably the only very small man in the Virginia Convention of 1776," he added.

Physiognomy: That's the word for it — for the direction this inquiry has taken me. The unknown, less than firm, terrain I'm now treading is no longer the familiar land of the Piedmont, but a form of psychohistory. Physiognomy, my dictionary says, is the discovery of temperament and character as revealed through outward appearance— not unlike, I suppose, a universal truth made manifest by a local landscape. And so the tall, athletically framed

Jefferson could afford to be idealistic, boldly so, and dare to pen the Declaration of Independence; and the small, frail Madison, by physical necessity cautious and exceedingly practical, crafted a Constitution that would protect even the weakest citizens. Perhaps neither man would have objected to this interpretation, for they both subscribed to a philosophical empiricism that meant ideas came from the sensation of experience. Does it then follow that the individual body perceiving the experience must inevitably and uniquely shape the idea?

To my knowledge, that particular question was one of the few never directly posed by Jefferson and Madison, as their unbounded curiosity tackled just about every issue imaginable having to do with human existence, the physical world, and the world beyond. Like heroic versions of Mutt and Jeff, their disparate physical appearances may have served only to make them alter egos, sharing the common ground of the Piedmont while joined together in the examined life of the mind. The voluminous, life-long correspondence between these friends and neighbors addressed everything from such weighty philosophical issues as whether "the earth belongs always to the living generation" (Jefferson said yes; Madison, a qualified no) to almost every observable physical detail of the earth itself. For example, to test his hypothesis that altitude and distance from the sea were the critical variables in determining the earth's temperature, Jefferson proposed recording simultaneous thermometer readings at Monticello,

Montpelier, and Annapolis. But the experiment apparently never took place; Madison didn't have the right thermometer.

Perhaps that was Madison's gentlemanly way of saying there were other, more pressing and practical tasks at hand. And I can hear Madison telling me, in the most polite manner, of course, that as a 20th-Century writer, I, too, don't possess the proper thermometer. This metaphorical thermometer has nothing to do with my word-processor or my access to source materials. Rather, I am asking questions that cannot be answered because they are wrongly framed. Neither personality and character nor beliefs and ideology can be objectively calibrated. There is no thermometer to the task. I should have known better, for there are no straight lines in the rolling Piedmont, no measurable cause and effect.

I had always assumed, for example, that the sometimes confused nature of U.S. foreign policy, about which our allies typically complain, owed its origins to the conflicting texts of the Declaration and the Constitution. From the idealism of the Declaration could be traced our diplomatic intolerance for "human rights abuses" in other countries; from the Constitution's pragmatic premise that humans are self-interested, our requirement that American foreign policy always be in "the national interest."

Now, on reflection, as if discovering once hidden details in a familiar landscape, I see that what I had thought to be competing ideologies are in fact intertwined and blur together. Just as there are no straight lines in the Piedmont, there is also no simplistic dialectic of either/or. Mountains and flatlands, like idealism and realism, fuse. And so it is that U.S. foreign policy is not so much confused as complex, like a split-personality: While lecturing many of the world's governments on how to treat their citizens, the representatives of we the American people have simultaneously and often looked the other way at gross violations of human rights under regimes considered geopolitically useful. Likewise, our professed idealism can lead to both isolationism (better than the rest of the world, we'll teach by example) and intervention (knowing what's best, we are obligated to work our will on others). And when we do act pragmatically out of perceived self-interest, as other nations do, we alone seem compelled to put an idealistic gloss to it, for example: "To make the world safe for democracy," said Woodrow Wilson when balance of power was the underlying issue; "aggression will not stand," said George Bush when the West's oil life-line was threatened.

So, too, as the landscape's hills blend and fade into one another, any real ideological differences between Madison and Jefferson blur and shift, rather than sharpen, if the Declaration and Constitution are read within the context of the 18th-Century Piedmont and not through the prism of today. The texts of the two documents express not opposing, but complementary, visions and personalities. If actions speak louder than words, look only at the political actions of the two men: Just as Jefferson sided with Madison against their fellow Virginian George Mason in the cause of a strong federal government, so Madison later parted political ways with Hamilton, his *Federalist Papers* partner.

The truth may be self-evident, but views of it, like those from Monticello and Montpelier, are forever nuanced. We the people can always lift a quote here and there from Jefferson and/or Madison, in order to legitimize our own particular point of view or political persuasion at the moment. And as for the Declaration and Constitution themselves — regardless of arguments about original intent, strict construction, or deconstruction — the fact is that each reader is apt to create his own text in the act of reading. The protean Jefferson, the protean Madison, changing but timeless, ever available to accommodate shifting political winds and sensibilities, like the seasons of the Piedmont that was their home. But the search for the authentic character of Jefferson and the eternal verities of Madison will continue always — inspiring endless books and essays such as this — as long as there is a nation called America, scriptures known as the Declaration and Constitution, and a Piedmont remembered as their land.

So to my puzzlement that first prompted this essay, I will answer with a question. The first question was: How could the same time and place, the same Piedmont landscape, produce both Jefferson and Madison and thus similarly inspire such very different texts as the Declaration and the

Constitution? My answer is the same reason that are "two" Homers. How could one mortal create such different but equally great works as the *Iliad* and the *Odyssey*? This question, too, has kept scholars and writers busy for centuries, and will continue as long as there's a civilization called Western.

Advocates and judges, scholars and theorists, go back to the text; I go back to the landscape. The land is like words; what they mean lies in how we use them. ❧

TO BUILD A CABIN

DON'T ask why. Although, like all stories, this one must have a beginning and an end, obsessions are another matter. So it is that I can remember with crisp, autumn clarity that October morning over 20 years ago when, with a pick and shovel, I broke ground on a small mountaintop overlooking Virginia's Blue Ridge, but cannot tell you why—or where the first impulse to build the cabin came from.

Child psychologists say the urge to manipulate space, to make private places in a public world, is innate, as evidenced by those mysterious mountains molded out of blankets in a nestling infant's crib. Whatever the roots, and their first cause, the cabin now seems simply to have sprouted from the forest floor.

If you didn't know where to look for it, you might not even see it. The sightseers in their Skyline Drive-bound autos, whom I can't help spying from the deck that hangs off the mountainside, don't notice, for the cabin's construction never broke the ridgeline. They don't know that I moved a mountain (or at least a small chunk of it) with a little (actually a lot of) help from my friends.

Sometimes I can't even believe I did it. Certainly, had I known then what I know now, I wonder whether I would ever have undertaken it—ever disturbed the earth there, a carpet of needles beneath a canopy of white pines, elevation 937 feet above sea level, right above a jagged outcropping of cold, gray, lichen-dotted rock ledges.

Maybe I'm not responsible; maybe the site made me do it. The land there was perfectly placed, the view it commanded as beautiful as it gets in this small corner of the natural world near Washington, DC, where I worked at the time. My gaze tumbled down the steep, forested incline to the middle distance of a lush patchwork of rolling, cultivated and cattle-grazed fields, only to be drawn upward to the hazy horizon of the gently powerful Blue Ridge. That's where the sun would set, and this is what my cantilevered deck and multi-paned casement windows would open onto. Who hasn't looked at a particular piece of land and conjured up a dream house? But most people are sufficiently wise, or simply prudent enough, not to act out their every fantasy. Still, mine wasn't an impossible dream, I thought: nothing so grand as an actual house, though neither so pedestrian and practical as mere shelter. A cabin. A cabin in the woods. There's magic in the words. So basic, so honest: a cabin that I would build with my own hands. So pure, so authentic: using only materials native to the land. So much fun, I guess is what I thought. Had I known what I was doing, it would have been work.

But once those first pick-and-shovel swings and scoops had scarred the earth, there was no turning back. As the hole for the cabin's foundation got deeper and deeper, and the pile beside it—fresh topsoil, then thick red clay, mixed with lots and loads of rocks—higher and higher, the once pristine site became suddenly ugly. Man had made his

mark. This was what ownership, not stewardship, of the land must mean. Not recording a deed in the county courthouse, but turning the soil, like fencing the boundaries, to make it yours somehow. If you didn't leave some mark, was it ever really yours? Were you even alive? Yes, he was alive once, they would say: See the futile, funny hole he dug

Yes, I would have to finish what I'd started, though the Saturdays extended into Sundays and the weekends turned into months of trying to fit my square hole into the round mountain. To really rape the land, you need a bulldozer; with mere hand tools, it had to be more like love, though unrequited. Each stroke of the mattock into the rocky soil felt like a mortal body blow. Not until the first snowfall had a neck-high (upslope), rectangular shelf, like an English basement, been carved into the mountainside. It was as level and straight as it would ever be. But it wasn't perfect. Nothing ever is, you may say, but, as any reputable builder will tell you, if your foundations aren't square and plumb, whatever you create will be crooked. Painfully crooked; I would spend endless future hours compensating for one wall a few inches too long and at least two corners not exactly 90 degrees. Curved space equals wasted time; the round mountain would always resist my linear will.

Everything took longer, more time than I'd ever imagined; likewise, I constantly underestimated the materials needed, overestimated the materials on hand. Had I been evaluated on plan-versus-actual performance, I would have had to fire myself. Plan, what plan? Although expectations (as in hopes and dreams) were plentiful, there was no plan. No architectural blueprint, no MBA-like business strategy. A plan would have meant that I knew what I was doing; and had I known what I was doing, really getting into....

But the cabin wasn't just in my head. I was constantly testing dimensions, proportions, scale and roof pitches with compass and ruler, pencil and paper. Doodles on restaurant napkins cluttered my pockets; just about every book ever published on house construction crowded my shelves; my desk at work in downtown Washington began to resemble a draftsman's tilted table. It helped that my office at the time overlooked Washington National Cathedral, still under construction. I daydreamed out my office window: Most true cathedrals took centuries to build.

Over the next couple of years, in fact, I made a point of becoming personally acquainted with some of the cathedral's master stonemasons. They chiseled the Indiana sandstone; I picked their brains. For I had decided to make my cabin—not out of straw, not out of glass—but from field stone, and stonemasonry is a dying art. When one of the Italian masons gave me a broken stone I treasured it like gold; it would serve as the humble cabin's grand cornerstone.

At first, I recycled the rocks I'd extracted in digging the foundation. When they ran out, I scoured the neighboring pastures — farmers, over the years, had actually done a lot of work for me by clearing the fields of stones, making neat piles where solitary trees now grew. The stones were free; so was my labor. All shapes, sizes, weights, textures and gradations of gray, they were loaded one at a time into the back of my Toyota Land Cruiser for the trip up the mountain.

Working with stone is like working with words.... Mortaring a row of irregular rocks is no different from constructing a sentence.... To write this story is to rebuild my stone cabin.... Words, like stones.... In the vocabulary of rocks, the choices are infinite. You create your own puzzle. One thing leads to another.

Crazy, said a doctor friend from the city, watching me and other friends lift the rocks, sometimes so heavy they required three or four of us to juggle them into the place. Solemnly talking about possible hernias and lower-back problems that could last for life, he refused to help. He never mentioned the carcinogens of creosote (since outlawed) we would splash on ourselves while liberally coating the log joists that would fit in the stone walls. Then we would smoke cigarettes to punctuate our progress. Otherwise, it must have been healthy.

"Better than psychotherapy," said more than one frequent visitor and slavelike laborer. "Better than spa activities," joked the proprietor of the building supply store where I bought the cement and sand that would be hand-mixed into the mortar that would hold the stones that would make the walls that would form the cabin.

What kind of world must Washingtonians live in when manual labor is considered rest and recreation? I didn't need to cajole or play Tom Sawyer to have a volunteer work gang every weekend, just as if I were having an old-fashioned barnraising. But it wasn't always a cooperative gang, since competitive instincts weren't necessarily ditched at the Beltway. fierce debates about the precise placement of stones disturbed the woodland's quiet; two friends, angling for the same job back in Washington, almost ended it all while pushing and pulling on a two-man saw; plans were made to set off the names of those who'd worked the most with a specially engraved flourish on a memorial brass plaque that would be inlaid above the fireplace.

A French colleague (in those early days I worked at the Washington Delegation for what's now the European Union) held the record for the most batches of mortar mixed in one day. fifteen wheelbarrows' worth she did— each requiring nine shovelsful of sand and three of cement, then stirred with a dash of water, as if a Continental pastry dough. At the end of the day, exhausted, she had to be almost carried down the mountain. Later that summer, when she returned to her Brussels headquarters, as a farewell gift and cabin-warming present she gave me Philip Slater's book *The Pursuit of Loneliness: American Culture at the Breaking Point.*

And so this pioneer-like cabin began to achieve a bit of transatlantic notoriety, as European visitors, taking a break from their official Washington duties, would insist on stopping by en route to Monticello. Both destinations, I was told, as if I were the unappreciative curator of a valued national treasure, were "uniquely American." The only similarity I could see, however, was that both occupied small mountaintops. And by now I well understood why most early American houses were built not on islandlike mountains but in more accessible hollows and valleys: Up the rough slope I had to transport not only stones, cement and sand but even the water to mix them.

Two members of the Palestine Liberation Organization delegation to the United Nations even stopped by once. They had to obtain special permission from the State Department to leave New York City to visit Amissville, Virginia. Savvy when it came to survival, they silently surveyed the site and then spoke their first words: "But where do you get your water?"

As for electricity, a sympathetic family member once gave me a gasoline-powered generator so power tools could transcend my pure but primitive construction methods. It is the only thing—knock on wood—that's ever been stolen from the cabin.

By the second year, as I started the fireplace and chimney, I had grown into a comfortable, slow-but-steady rhythm. The mortar dripped less; I could eyeball a rock and tell whether it would fit without having to lift, heave, and test it; engineer and architect friends who had initially scoffed now just shook their heads in awe at my perhaps admirable (but still stupid) determination. "What you've built could withstand a nuclear bomb blast," they said. Yes, it was true, I had overbuilt; the form did not follow function. But maybe it wasn't meant to be just a simple cabin after all—maybe not a cathedral exactly, but "some kind of monument to immortality," said a well-respected Richmond architect, laughing. But stone ruins would be the ultimate end of all my work, I knew. Even then, at the beginning, that's what I'd created, according to the surveyor I'd commissioned to plot my land. He didn't know I was building a cabin; stumbling upon it in the woods, he'd carefully pinpointed it on the final survey: "Stone ruins." I didn't get angry.

Today, though, topped as it is with a shingle roof and dormer windows, no one would call my cabin a ruin. But neither is it complete. After the stonework, the rest—the framing, the trimming—was easy. Perhaps too easy, for I didn't—and still don't—work as hard. I began to cheat, using not hand-hewn but store-bought lumber. There's always something to do, particularly now that the more mortal materials, like wooden window sills, need repair. Sometimes I think out loud about starting another, bigger house, for which the cabin would be the guest quarters. People around me look at me as if I'm crazy: Why, the cabin's not even finished!   But that's the point, I guess. The 19th-Century German romantics had a phrase for it—*immer wird, nie ist* (always becoming, never is). I know now that the goal *was* the process. The cabin should never be finished—and it never will be. Still, to say I have no regrets would make me a liar. Would I do some things differently? Certainly. But stone, once set in mortar, cannot be easily moved. Pure justice was in the moment: Either I did it right or I did it wrong, and I have to live with what I did—the crooked wall, the jagged, out-of-place rock right above the mantle, the....

The past hardens like mortar, and sometimes, I confess, while watching the sun set from my deck whose boards now need restraining, I wonder whether there were better things I could have done with my time than build this cabin. Just about the same year I dug up the first rock on the mountain, for example, Little Rock's Bill Clinton began his own obsessive building toward the White House. But then I think, the view from my cabin—of autumn leaves, not November elections—has got to be better. ❧

APOLOGIA FROM AMISSVILLE

AMISSVILLE is no Katmandu. Still, there's a ring to it, this name for an out-of-the-way, Virginia foothills hamlet. It makes you want to take a trip. You can visualize the place without ever having been there, even without knowing where it is on the map exactly. And what you see in your mind's eye is pretty much what you'd get. For me to offer a detailed description of the place would therefore be unnecessary, and might even disappoint. But I will tell you about my own trip, a pilgrimage really, about how I arrived at Amissville. Although it is only 20 miles or so from where I grew up, the journey is not short. The road has turns and switchbacks, and only in retrospect is the destination clear.

This journey, as with life itself, starts with sex. It sells, the marketers tell us. *Sex and Canoeing* should have been the title of Randy Carter's *River Guide*, I remember Randy's joking whenever he was asked about the book's sales. At the time, the 1960s, his was a lone voice in the Eastern wilderness seeking to preserve what was left of it. Now, 25 years after his death, the Virginia rivers Randy cherished have more people paddling them than he would ever have imagined — and thus wanting to preserve them, too.

My point, I think, is that nature and history are now, and only recently, positive and marketable themes in American popular culture. Perhaps it has something to do with advertisers' emphasis on value, the public's acceptance of notions like recycling, the service and information economy, or the approaching Millennium; but whatever the cause(s), things that last sell. Certainly, this has not always been the case, at least in my lifetime, in the years since mid-century. If it was new, it was good, and big was always better. Planned obsolescence was the business strategy of the auto industry, whose manufacturing base was the business of America. (Randy drove a Volkswagen.)

This same point became clear, I also think, after the dust had settled from the battle over the planned Disney America theme park, a defining event for Virginia's Piedmont. It was not simply a land-use question about yet more suburban sprawl, pitting the usual suspects in the pro- and anti-growth, progress-versus-preservation debate. Rather, the terms of the debate were fundamentally changed. The question was no longer whether to destroy the past in order to make way for the future but how best to appreciate, use, and/or exploit the past. The shared value was history; the difference was whose version, whose interpretation of history?

The battle was between popularizers and purists. As such, the repudiation of Disney's celebratory vision of America's heritage marked an interesting chapter in the so-called culture wars — between elitists and philistines, hi-brow and low-brow, or as the British say, U and non-U. As Disney's formidable collection of opponents demonstrated, one doesn't have to be rich to be an elitist, not even well-educated. All that's required is contentment with the status quo, and a willingness to defend it. The

popularizers are the aggressors, and they have numbers on their side, just as General Grant did in another invasion of Virginia. Like Grant, eventually they'll win what is really a war of resources and attrition as long as they retain the numerical advantage. For in a democracy, the majority — embodying not only power but also moral virtue — is supposed to triumph. So, too, is the marketplace that efficiently responds to mass desire. But victory is seldom clear-cut or total; such is the nature of democratic compromise.

I doubt the preservationists realized it at the time, but even if they had lost the Disney battle, they already had pretty much won the war. For in today's America, just about everyone buys into — or at least gives lip service to — the country's past. Like any of Disney's fantasy creations, heritage is an idea that sells. The more creative the packaging — a marketing euphemism for abridged, adulterated, or compromised — the brisker the sales. But you no longer have to be a preservationist or an elitist to buy it.

Randy Carter was an elitist — in the most Virginian sense of that word. An FFV (first Families of Virginia), he felt honored to have both Carters and Randolphs in his blood. Yet he also became popular, much to the surprise of him and his stepson (me). His canoeing book would eventually go into seven printings; and well-thumbed, dog-eared copies, though now long out of print, can still be spotted on the seats and dashboards of canoe-and-kayak-topped Jeeps and other fashionable, four-wheel-drive vehicles as they ply Virginia's historic backroads in search of unspoilt nature's rushing waters.

Meanwhile, the Piedmont Environmental Council, which had led the fight against Disney, quickly capitalized on its moment in the sun — by promoting, for example, a coffee-table book with lavish color photographs of the Piedmont's storied landscape. The price to consumers was about the same as an admission ticket to Disney World. I'm sure the book's photographers would take issue with my analogy, for they no doubt view themselves as more artists than entertainers — and their work as created especially for the appreciative few.

Few or many, we each exploit the past in our own way. This past includes, of course, the Piedmont landscape, whose form and function we inherit from our predecessors.

"The past is not dead. It isn't even past." To quote (exploit) William Faulkner, I simply mean to say that the past is Protean; we work it to our will, meeting our needs of the moment. We define ourselves as individuals to the degree we accept, rebel against, or feel imprisoned by the past. And so collectively, the popular culture is defined.

In recent years the images in our heads of the gentry good life, and its romance of the past, make Piedmont Virginia a desirable place to live — and preserve. When I was growing up here, most of the people I knew wanted to leave; progress was still deemed good, and by definition that meant turning your back on the place, and the past it represented. Now the place has new value, created by the

demand of the newcomers. The supply of land is limited, so Piedmont real estate prices rise.

Value. Demand. Supply. Prices. These are terms of the marketplace, and they now read like highway directional signs enroute to Amissville. This is by way of saying that I haven't forgotten where I was going, the purpose of this piece. But 20 some years ago, I must now admit, I had not the slightest idea where I was ultimately headed — and that I would at this moment be writing a justification for the road, including byways and detours, my life has taken. This, then, is my apologia from Amissville.

Comprising a country store, a church, a firehouse, a post office, and a few family dwellings set alongside Route 211, Amissville can not be said to have the status even of a crossroads village, yet for me it has come to symbolize the often hazardous intersection of art and commerce — and of the warring sides of my own divided self. In the publishing world, where I've spent most of my professional life, this division is usually formalized into a Church-and-State-like separation between the Ivory Tower of writing and editing and the Black Tower of advertising and other business concerns. Amissville is where I crossed the line.

In the early 1970s, when Piedmont land was still relatively cheap, I bought a few acres near Amissville. It would be my weekend refuge from the world of Washington, where I worked at the time. Sunday after Sunday evening, returning from the country, I unhappily discovered a slow but steady increase in traffic. The fact that the people in these cars impeding my way must be doing the same thing as I only made me unhappier. There was nothing I could do to stop them, so then the thought occurred: Why not launch a publication designed especially for them?

And so *Country* magazine was conceived, at least the idea of it. To make it happen required capital that I didn't have, other people's money. To sell the idea to investors, I armed myself with market research, polling data, direct-mail test results, focus group studies, whatever it took to quantify my emotional hunch. Only later did I learn that what actually sold them was my enthusiasm for the editorial concept. It was expressed like so:

"All these people are coming out to the countryside. I personally don't want them to come, but I can't stop them. The paradox, indeed the danger, is that they will, in their sheer numbers, destroy the very thing that attracted them in the first place. So we'll provide the useful information they want and will pay for — about country property, country inns, things to do and see — but presented in such a way as to convert them into preservationists and environmentalists. We won't be shrill or obvious about it; otherwise, we'd end up just preaching to the choir. Rather, we'll seduce them into a sense of appreciation for the region's history and natural beauty."

The investors were well aware that the failure rate for new magazines is about the same as for restaurants, and so we were all most pleasantly surprised when *Country* quickly attracted a loyal subscriber base, with traditionally cautious advertisers soon following. We were even more surprised — shocked is more like it — when, after publishing only 18 monthly issues, we received one of those proverbial offers you can't refuse. It was from another, much larger media company, headed by Reg Murphy — who later went on to gain some notoriety espousing his core belief that "profit is not a dirty word" as the first outside president and CEO of the venerable National Geographic Society. In addition to the substantial monetary return to the original investors who had trusted and believed in me, I liked the idea because of Reg's commitment both to invest even more money in circulation growth and to allow me to continue running the magazine, including its editorial direction, however I wished. The bottomline would be his only interest.

I also liked the idea because I liked Reg. His reputation was that of a ruthless, cold-blooded manager and turn-around artist who treated all subordinates as dispensable in his quest to increase shareholder value. "You're just about the only person in the whole organization who doesn't fear Reg," a publishing executive confided in me one day as we both waited outside the forbidding doors of the directors' boardroom at corporate headquarters in Baltimore. But in my own relationship with Reg, friendship was easily substituted for fear, I think now in retrospect, because of our shared sense of place. Reg had grown up in Georgia's hill country — the "Pigmont," I would tease him. Over restaurant lunches of Brunswick stew, we would playfully argue over the name's derivation: the Brunswick on the seacoast of Georgia or the Brunswick of southside Virginia. We would only agree that the Georgian version of Brunswick stew contained fricasseed squirrel, eyeballs and tail included.

This is not to say we never talked business. It flavored our conversation. I should write the way we talked, and then talk about what I wrote, Reg would suggest in his softest Southern manner: "I don't mean to tell you what to do, you're doing it so well already, and you know better than I, but I suspect that lots of good things would happen if you'd consider...." Specifically, his point, when he would finally get to it, was for me to inject my own personality in ever more obvious ways into the magazine, and then hit the road to publicize it. A good editor has to be a marketer, he would beguile me — again in the softest Southern way. And lo and behold, I would soon find myself, as kind of an awkward male version of Martha Stewart, booked on radio and television talk shows, from Winston-Salem to Philadelphia.

I would continue, nonetheless, to resist his frequent suggestion that I might want to write a publisher's letter to the readers each month to introduce that issue's contents. Many, if not most, magazines had such "Dear Reader" columns, usually packaged with a picture of the publisher or editor, with tie loosened, sleeves rolled up, and pencil in hand. They reminded me of politicians' campaign flyers. I had always disdained such public posturing in print and

doubted that any readers except other editors and publishers ever paid much attention. And I told Reg so; and he persisted in his gentle way. He never gave direct orders, although those who feared him would say that any suggestion of his was indeed an order and that one had better listen carefully to his quiet voice because such a suggestion was made only once. But in the case of this particular suggestion, it became a standing joke between us — "Have you written that publisher's letter yet?" he would greet me — as if he were playing a publicity agent and I, his self-effacing client.

One deadline night, as the next issue was about to go to press, I relented. Perhaps it was inevitable that this good Southern boy, who I was, would inevitably defer to Reg's authority. Or, maybe more accurately, I was simply keyed up with now nothing to do, and I was curious: let's have a go and see what happens. To begin with, I wouldn't run my picture, have my name in lights, or even to call it a "Publisher's Letter." Instead, I found myself punching the keys on my ancient typewriter to say "Letter From Amissville," even though I was sitting at my cluttered desk in the magazine's Alexandria office at the time. The column wasn't about me but about the place that had inspired the magazine's creation — and about how the view from my small mountaintop cabin there informed the contents of that magazine issue now going to bed.

Soon I grew to look forward to these monthly 500-word "Letters From Amissville" — and, much to my surprise and delight, so did the readers. Their letters to me flowed; paid circulation grew to over 100,000; renewal rates increased to 70 percent; Reg's bottomline looked ever better; and even today, long after I 'm gone from the magazine and its ownership has changed hands, people whom I don't know tell me they miss the word from Amissville.

I miss Amissvlle too. It had come to represent a place of precarious balance in my professional life, midway between the Charybdis of impractical dreamer and the Scylla of shallow businessman. In my college days I had felt a joyous affinity with William ("Count No-Count") Faulkner's response when fired from his job as postal clerk that he "had refused to be at the beck and call of anybody who could afford a two-cent stamp." On the other hand, in my own first real jobs, I was equally disdainful of my fellow writers who never understood and weren't even mildly curious about the source of their salaries, though they were the quickest to complain if their paychecks were the slightest bit late. I suppose this split personality helps explain why I'm neither a critically acclaimed novelist nor a titan of commerce. Instead, the dreamer in me dared to imagine creating a magazine; and the business side of me had made it work. Everything had come together; my divided self was whole for a time.

Who doesn't want to have one's cake and eat it, too? In what seems now almost an imaginary place called Amissville, that happened for me. And the place and I

were as one, for celebrating the history and natural beauty it came to represent was shown to be not necessarily incompatible with making a buck.

Not long after Amissville disappeared from the magazine, the publication's name was changed to *Mid-Atlantic Country*. Gradually and progressively, during a succession of different publishers and art directors, the "Mid-Atlantic" typography became bigger, bolder and the "Country" smaller, fainter. It was a mistake, I think, although I understand why it was done — to make buying decisions easier and more likely for national advertisers and agencies. By signaling that the publication was a slick regional, it would be differentiated from all the other "country" magazines — *Country Living, Country Homes, Country Life,* etc. And the ad dollars did soon flow, targeting the region's desirable demographics. But circulation suffered; then, in a slow but inevitable spiral, advertising fell off too. Indeed, as I write this, exactly 20 years after the inaugural issue, the magazine's newest owners have notified creditors that its bills can no longer be paid.

To me, it feels like a child has died.

"You have to grow or die," Reg Murphy used to tell me in our talks about the magazine's future. But growth, too, can kill. In fact, it's an old, too typical story that once a small business loses its personal, entrepreneurial imprint, it often flounders. The customers — in this case, the readers — sense something is amiss. At the risk of oversimplifying the many variables in a successful publishing equation, I suspect that most readers never much cared for the word "Mid-Atlantic." It was hard to find even in an dictionary. The name sounds like it's describing the middle of the ocean. There exists no historical usage, thus no rich, emotion-laden connotations. It's a marketer's moniker, not authentic like Amissville. "I'm a Mid-Atlantan," says no one, in contrast to the currency and fluency of "I'm a Virginian/Southerner/Yankee." But, I must confess, now I see this clumsy geographic designator everywhere — even the TV weathermen talk about rain and sunshine in the Mid-Atlantic. Years from now, I hope the lexicographers will give my old magazine the credit it deserves. Or blame.

In any case, Amissville will remain just as it is on the map — still no more than a tiny dot, I hope. Nowhere else could be more place specific yet at the same time evocative of so much more. "Amissville" as metonymy or synecdoche for "Country," my column's headline and the magazine's title were interactive without being wired, inviting the reader's imagination to play. That's why so many people subscribed to my magazine and looked forward to its publisher's letters, I guess now in retrospect. The magazine was, as they say in the publishing trade, a dream book, transporting the mostly urban and suburban readers to a land of make-believe that may have existed only in the past. Somewhere in the country, perhaps a place called Amissville. ❧

BATTLEFIELDS ON A MYTHICAL LANDSCAPE

"Let us cross over the river and rest under the
shade of the trees."
    —*Thomas Jonathan "Stonewall" Jackson's dying words*

"Lewis B. Puller, Jr.— the son of 'Chesty' Puller, a hero of
World War II and the Korean War — grew up in a family
whose strongest tradition was that of serving one's country.
Upon graduation from William and Mary College at the
height of the Vietnam War, young Lewis almost inevitably
joined the Marine Corps.... A few months later, he returned home to his wife and soon-to-be-born child missing
his left leg above the knee, his right leg at the torso, most
of his left hand, and a thumb and a finger of his right
hand."
    — *From the dustjacket of the 1991 autobiography*
    Fortunate Son: The Healing of a Vietnam Vet,
    by Lewis B. Puller, Jr., who committed suicide in 1994

THE hot, humid, muggy, and buggy summers along
the Rappahannock River, where Stonewall Jack
son died and where Lewis B. Puller, Jr. grew up,
make some of us think of Vietnam. Like most Virginia
boys, Lewis Puller learned early and by heart Jackson's last,
dream-like command, his deathbed words after the Battle
of Chancellorsville. Mistaken for the enemy, shot and
mortally wounded by his own men, Jackson's death too
was a kind of suicide.

It occurred at 3 p.m. on May 10, 1863.

Although Lew Puller was a friend of mine, I have no idea whether he was aware that it was almost exactly 131 years later, even to the hour, when on that May day of 1994 he pulled the trigger to take his own life. I do know — from his Pulitzer Prize-winning memoir *Fortunate Son* — that in his boyhood, he had invoked Robert E. Lee's and Stonewall Jackson's "hallowed names in my bedtime prayers before my father tucked me in."

Lew's father and namesake was Lewis B. "Chesty" Puller, a general of mythic proportions, the most highly decorated officer in Marine Corps history, whose own grandfather had been killed at Kelly's Ford, like Chancellorsville, a Civil War battleground on the banks of the Rappahannock.

Kelly's Ford. Chancellorsville. Brandy Station. Fredericksburg. Ball's Bluff. Manassas. The mere mention of these Piedmont placenames, attached forever to sites of Civil War clashes, seemed to send a shiver down the spines of boys like Lew and me. We were not what today would be called "Civil War buffs." History was not a hobby; it was who we were, in our blood. The orders of battle, the names and personalities of commanders, and the decisive moments of action in each battle — we knew by heart. Reenactments with tin soldiers were more than toys and games; they were an expression of the South's collective consciousness and an exploration into the mysterious realm of "what if" and "what might have been."

What if Longstreet had been less cautious.... What if Jackson had not been killed....

Clinically speaking, what killed Lew Puller, the great-grandson of a Confederate casualty at Kelly's Ford, was a self-inflicted gunshot wound — and probably the lingering effects of painkilling medications. Another painkiller with which Lew had probably been too familiar was alcohol. Like other Southern boys, Lewis was introduced to both guns and drink at an early age. Like a bad metaphor, guns give the illusion of power and control: to work the world to your will when the world as you find it is wrong, so different from the world you imagined and expected. But when the world doesn't change, alcohol lubricates the painful friction, the constant grinding, as powerful as that of the earth's tectonic plates, between what was and what is, what might have been and what really wasn't.

It's easy, and probably not wrong, to say that Lew Puller died from the unhealed wound he suffered in Vietnam. What's harder to argue — but I will — is that he also died from the stories we tell ourselves, the myths necessary to nation-building, and a present so incongruous that the past seems a lie.

Imagine the unthinkable: that a once familiar, tranquil landscape, like that carved by the Rappahannock, and the history associated with it, is suddenly, violently, and irretrievably altered, even erased, by a catastrophic geological event. The Blue Ridge flattened; to the east a volcano or two in place of peacefully rolling pasture land;

a parched desert where once grew lush, deciduous trees; no river running through it. Your world turned upside down.

What did you do in the war, Daddy? That's the question all Baby Boomers asked of the generation that had borne them. The war we were talking about was, of course, World War II. Its crystal-clear, black-and-white images, to linger forever in our psyches, were everywhere: the movies we saw, the games we played. Even the first President most of us remember was the D-Day commander who had liberated Europe. Emotion-laden names, like Operation Overlord and Omaha Beach, still ring like magic. We celebrated their 50th anniversary that June in the year of Lew Puller's suicide.

But about our own war in our own time, what would we tell our children? Vietnam was "different," is just about all we can say. And so to our children, the so-called Generation Xers, Lew Puller must seem to be their parents' Kurt Cobain.

We the parents still don't have our stories straight. How can we explain that some of us, like Lew Puller, volunteered bravely to serve, while others, like myself, served reluctantly and luckily (I was shipped to Europe, not Vietnam) or, like Bill Clinton, who as President must symbolize the country's past and future, gladly didn't serve at all?

That's where despair lies, I think: where there's no explanation, no simple story that satisfies, no controlling theme. Does that mean that the stories our own parents told us were lies? Were we stupid to believe? Just to ask the questions causes pain. Or maybe the stories of Civil War gallantry and World War II righteousness weren't false exactly; but our own lives, our time on this earth, turned them into lies?

The world that the Vietnam generation inherited was not supposed to work the way it did. America was supposed to win its wars, or at least have the will to do so. But if it didn't, as Southerners were taught and learned the lesson of their Lost Cause, the defeat was honorable. No one ever died— giving one's life for one's country — in vain. The ones who survived were heroes; the more heroic, the greater the wounds. They were noble, victorious, successful in everything they did even if there were no victory parades. They did not lose elections to draft-dodgers, as Lew Puller unapologetically called the man who beat him in a 1978 Virginia congressional race. "I despised him," wrote Puller, "for having been spared the most catastrophic episode of our generation."

Yet years later at Washington's Vietnam Memorial Wall, in an inspired gesture to heal the nation's wounds, if not his own, he moved his wheel-chair shoulder-to-shoulder with Bill Clinton to face down the boos directed at the draft-dodging President by Puller's fellow veterans. To the end, Puller was the good soldier, always did his duty.

That was on a Memorial Day, what Southerners mourning their Lost Cause once called Decoration Day. Survivors and descendants would decorate the tombstones of the fallen — so by way of saying, "We'll never forget."

Wars are never over, they say. Witness the Palestinians and Israelis, the Bosnian Serbs and Muslims, who have been fighting forever, it seems. But even if and when the guns stop firing, the images do indeed last forever. And it is those timeless memories that form us, make us the individuals we are, the nation we have conceived. So Lew Puller's story is now a feature in the landscape of our memory.

"The lessons learned from Vietnam." We hear that refrain a lot, particularly when the politicians argue or the historians tell us what America is and who We The People are. But simply to remember Lewis Puller and his courageous wheel-chaired image, that's enough for me. That's the kind of storytelling that leads to true nation-building, for future generations to know their legacy is not a lie.

Like Lee, Jackson, and his father "Chesty," the name of Lewis B. Puller, Jr. is hallowed now—his story true. He is resting under the shade of the trees, just as Stonewall ordered. The grave is in the Arlington National Cemetery, once General Lee's family home. And when I cross the Rappahannock or even the Styx, I will remember Lew Puller — more than a myth, a human being. ❧

Trespassing on the Land of the Body

FLIMSY and filmy, the clouds bringing the first showers of spring floated across and then draped the Blue Ridge in layered veils of gauzy chiffon and cobwebbed georgette, as I sat on the stone wall watching the sunset. I contemplated the sheer textures, the shadows, and the shades of darkness and of meaning — cobalt, gray, silver on the edge of black. Coming ever closer, the clothes of clouds transformed the mountains' mass into a seductively moving body, gliding, even swishing with exaggerated femininity. And right where the sun should be the clouds turned into shreds of bright pink and purplish blue, like the bruised and sutured flesh hidden by my bandages.

Although I wrote those words, they don't belong to me. They reflect the voice of a character I recently created in a novel in progress, likely to remain forever unfinished. But the voice sometimes sounds more like that of a Frankenstein monster than of any real-life person I know, I often think when reworking the prose. This character, the first-person narrator, is supposed to be a woman, not fully formed, so a girl really. But she sometimes sounds more like a burlesque caricature, even a postoperative transsexual; this would explain "the bruised and sutured flesh" that her bandages hide, wouldn't it? You'll have to read the novel to know for sure; but first, of course, I have to finish it — to know myself.

What I can never know for sure is what it's like, what it means, how it feels, to be a woman. Or, more particularly, what would I be like if I were a woman? Besides the obvious transformation in outward appearance, how in fact would I be different? How would my world then change? Forever trapped in a man's body, I can only observe and guess. To experience the being of oppositeness can never be existential. The body may be frail, but it is defining. A transvestite knows only the otherness of what clothes the object of his desire. A feminine boy, teased by his peers, knows the fearful boundaries of gender. Playfully, brazenly crossing those boundaries, a drag queen knows that life's a stage. But what a woman knows, a man can never find the words for.

Still, some of us try. What is writing if not empathic role-playing? It's fun, this play, to escape the bonds of, if not earth, our own bodies — with consequences no grander, no more irreversible, than trying on a Halloween mask. Words can be erased, false starts corrected, first drafts discarded. But, trying and trying, we know we'll never get it exactly right. Were we truly committed to truth, if not beauty, we would bravely submit ourselves as candidates for the medical procedure known as sex-reassignment. But a true sex-change, of the surgical kind, can not be unchanged. One can not, as in the title of that old television show, simply be "a queen for a day." Never a first, exploratory draft, a sex-change operation is the final cut.

The final cut: Why do we invariably resort to puns and snickers, hiding behind humor, when confronted with transsexualism? Such transmogrification frightens, such revolutionary change disturbs, to be sure. But also it is arguably truly transcendental. So, instead of the laughter of the freak show, something like the smile of beatitude might be more in order.

If we're serious and honest, we must surely admit that a true sex-change, this medical marvel, this modern miracle, engenders awe and fascination: God-like, to sculpt the body of your choice, to reflect the anima of your soul, to create yourself anew; indeed — if you're heterosexual — to know narcissistically, to possess at last, even to become the very object of your own desire. The problem (not the only one) is that the men who thus "become" women must apparently have motives more complex than either simple curiosity or the grandest truth-seeking. They suffer (clinical psychologists never say "enjoy") from gender dysphoria; the sex-change operation and accompanying hormonal therapy are corrective not cosmetic, remedial not reincarnating; few transsexuals claim to be Faustian creatures driven by the mysterious powers of Goethe's Eternal Feminine leading them forever onward.

A related but far more consequential problem in my own particular case is this: To discover what I would be like as a woman through sex-reassignment surgery, I realize that I would in effect be required to kill myself. Since my identity is so interwined with "being a man," my fear would thus be not simply of castration but of death itself. With the death of my former self, I would no longer be a participant-observer writer exploring the boundaries of gender but, by definition, a different person altogether. To be resurrected as this new person would have required a self-hatred so strong I might as well have been dead anyway — or at least a desire for knowledge so passionate and so courageous (foolhardy) as to have been self-destructive. Like committing suicide to find out if there's an after-life.

And there's the practical problem, as well: No matter how perfectly genitals can be reconstructed, breasts augmented, facial hair electrolyzed, or estrogen ingested, a postoperatve transsexual is not a genetic girl, never was, therefore never will be. The chromosomes are wrong. Transsexuals' reference in secret shorthand to genetic girls as GG's may sound like a giggly put-down, but it's bound to be envy. Venus envy. The condition of fertility, the possibility of bringing new life into the world, and of course childbirth itself, a transsexual can never know.

In this sense, all writers are would-be women. We can at least birth a novel — or an essay. We write not only what we know but also what we want to know. To write, perhaps even more than to read, is to learn. And so in my novel I find myself writing in the first-person feminine — following, perhaps presumptuously, in the tradition of Defoe's *Moll flanders* and Richardson's *Pamela*, both wonderfully scandalous in their time.

Stone is easier to work than flesh, I write. By grounding this observation in the rock outcroppings of the Piedmont's landscape, which I know, I can explore other, unfamiliar ways of seeing. I can myself become metamorphic, a modern Tiresias. Only after Tiresias was blinded could he truly see; and only after he was transformed into a woman were the greatest truths revealed to him. This Greek mythological figure's real-life equivalent — what anthropologists term the American Indians' "berdache" — no doubt moved through this very landscape. A kind of third gender, though anatomically male, berdaches combined behavioral characteristics of both men and women. They were revered as all-knowing archetypes of wholeness.

It is no accident, I think, that all primitive religions and pagan cultures extract magical transformations from nature. Polytheism and polymorphism go hand in hand. Even Christianity has its transubstantiation. If bread and wine can become body and blood, why shouldn't a man want to know what it's like to become a woman? Surely there's a spiritual unity in that? If Aphrodite can bring Pygmalion's stone statue to life, if the Greek youth called Narcissus can "morph" into a flower, why shouldn't I be intellectually curious about what it's like to be desired by me? That is, to experience true possession, to become the idealized woman whose body is desired by me?

Just to ask such questions is the societal, if not moral, equivalent of brazenly ignoring "no trespassing" signs posted along the well defined fencelines of the rural Virginia landscape. In the Piedmont, like the rest of the Old South, one is taught to know one's place. But another

Southern tradition is rebellion; and the Piedmont, perhaps more so than anywhere else, inspires transgression of boundaries. Neither mountainous nor flat, the Piedmont's rolling hills represent betweeness, a place of transition. Neither male nor female, transsexuals are said by psychologists "to be in transition" when living full-time in the gender to which they aspire preparatory to the sex-change surgery.

In today's religion of rationality, science, and commerce, if a developer can bulldoze and carve up the Piedmont landscape, why shouldn't a surgeon take a scalpel to my body? The goals seem similar: The land is made more accessible; and I gain access to once forbidden knowledge. But in making the land accessible, is it destroyed, just as changing the sex of my body would no doubt kill my former self? Or if not destroyed, the land is so altered that it is no longer desirable — just as if the sex of my body were to be its only change, would the woman that I thus become (neither young nor nubile) ever have been desired by the former me?

It's a connection that I find endlessly intriguing: the landscape and the human body. Is the way we perceive and experience the endless expressions of the earthly body that we call home influenced by the form and function of our own bodies, whether male or female — a dualism possibly as profound as the Cartesian mind-body? Why, for example, do I feel compelled to use words I normally would never use to describe a Blue Ridge sunset when adopting the voice of a female narrator? Or am I being simply sexist to assume the words should be different at all?

It is dangerous ground to tread, I realize, in more ways than one. The ground not only is a landscape, but has become a political arena as well. And the questions I raise are therefore not simply about words, but about power. On such battlegrounds of the so-called gender wars, even seemingly natural allies — for example, women and those men who want to be women — can become enemies. There's no hope of finding common ground, much less a common language, when a transsexual's worshipful and careful emulation is dismissed as ridiculous parody.

Dismissal, that's the usual reaction — from women and men alike — to any man who is curious enough to care to learn the difference between froufrou and toutou, who masters with authority a phrase like "fuchsia tuft of tulle" (to describe Opening Night Barbie's headpiece), or who knows that a lady's slipper, blooming on the Piedmont's hillsides, is also called hare's lip, old goose, camel's foot, ram's head, and Slipper of Our Lady. Such a man is seldom taken seriously.

Yet his gender-barrier-breaking soul sister — learning the once secret argot of the formerly all-male rat line at the Virginia Military Institute, for instance — is considered a brave champion for equal rights. To deride her with dismissive laughter is reactionary or worse. It's unfair and unjust, this new inequality, whereby a woman's world is constantly being widened while that which is uniquely woman's remains off-limits for anyone not genitally correct. GG's only need apply.

I just don't get it, obviously. I know. That I don't get it, I don't need to be reminded by female friends or you the reader. Parenthetically, I wonder just who are you, the readers of essays, anyway? Demographically speaking, what are your vital statistics? What percentage men, women? In another time, but still not too long ago, I could assume that very few pretty heads would be reading these words, and so would not have worried about coarsening feminine sensibilities with plot-less, character-less, and possibly amoral abstractions. Today, however, I must prudently assume the opposite — that you the reader are female — according to book publishers' sales statistics about who their audience is. Since books are knowledge, and knowledge is power, ignorance is no longer a requirement to be alluringly feminine. But if women are now plodding through tomes of philosophy and physics, why aren't men ravagingly devouring romance novels and fashion magazines? It smacks a bit of reverse discrimination, a new double standard.

On the subject of fashion magazines, I must confess to stealing a furtive look occasionally. The articles on the newest styles are as descriptive and evocative as the very best in nature writing, I've come to believe; after discovering the Paris shows through the words of a *Vogue*, *Elle*, or *Harper's Bazaar* reporter, for instance, the pastels of an April in Virginia will never be the same again. And the ads, I like them best: In their celebration of beautified bodies and the cyclical nature of time (clothes and makeup are, of course, seasonal), perhaps only a painter of Piedmont landscapes can compare. If linear time is addressed at all, it goes backwards, reversed into a new and younger you. All manner of boldly magical transformations are available to even the most self-effacing reader at the mere flip of a page, awakening normally repressed desires for wildest fantasy and endless possibility — you can become whoever you want to be. Imagine. As for the editor's photo layouts of stunning women, yes, I admit I stop and stare, unlike the proverbial *Playboy* reader who claims he buys the magazine only for its serious fiction.

Clearly, I lied: I do more than "steal a furtive look occasionally" at women's magazines. I read them all the time, but I seldom buy them; my wife does that. They are *her* magazines. I want to make that distinction clear. She doesn't mind sharing, nor would any other woman I know. The problem is men, myself included, who have a habit of confusing sex with gender. I don't want the checkout boy at the magazine store to make a pass at me. Fashion magazines, romance novels, froufrous, and fuchsia tufts of tulle are women's prerogatives in men's eyes only. To trespass into such feminine territory must make a man, by definition, not a man at all.

And so it is taboo, this forbidden knowledge. But a woman can enter what was formerly men-only domain with no such stigma. While few men would feel comfortable checking out a book from the public library on the art of maquillage (or even confess to care what it means), nowadays a woman can read all about carburetor repair with nary an eyebrow raised. Indeed, today's parents encourage their tottling daughters to play with toy cars and trains, in order to introduce them to the gender-free world of possibilities now in front of them; conversely, a baby boy displaying the slightest interest in dolls or dress-up is automatically suspect and cause for parental alarm. It's fine for a woman to don either skirts or pants, at her whim; but unless a man has a cultural okay such as his Scottish heritage, a skirt will never do. Even the most masculine attire on some women seems, paradoxically, to accentuate her sexuality, while the androgynous look on a man makes him as asexual as a eunuch.

This inequality about which I'm harping, my feminist friends point out, is entirely men's own doing; it reflects the fear, even hatred, of females by males in our society. When I counter that males love females, I'm told again that I just don't get it. But to keep saying that "I don't get it" argues my point precisely: Men don't get it, because they don't understand; they don't understand because men *are* different from women. But I do want to get it, to know, to see the world through the eyes of a woman, to be queen for as many days as it takes to write my novel, to go where no man has ever gone and come back a man to tell about it.

Even the most angry feminists and their equally angry adversaries agree that there do exist well-documented gender differences in the way we talk — and thus, as a corollary, in the way we think and see things. Equality doesn't necessarily require blurring differences to the point of androgyny. "Separate but equal," though the phrase comes from the old segregationist South, is a politically correct description of men and women's language differences — so different in fact that sociolinguistic scholars treat communication between the sexes as cross-cultural. So men and women in effect agree to disagree, to agree that we have inevitable misunderstandings. What nobody seems to agree on is the degree to which these differences are genetically or environmentally determined.

I (together with my female persona) will say this about that: The landscapes we grow up in must surely influence the way we react to and address the world. I am who I am because I'm a child of the rolling hills, cultivated and pastured, of Virginia. Had I grown up in an immense, flat land whose boundless horizons diminish the individual human figure (say, the steppes of Russia) or in a mountain hollow surrounded by dense, impenetrable forests (as dark and deep as Appalachian coal mines), my sense of self would inevitably have been altered. By the same token, I must also be who I am because of my own personal, private landscape — my body.

To explore further this notion of what I'll call bodyscape, what is the appropriately correct discipline — biology, geology, psychology, sociology — or is it interdisciplinary like that new curriculum called women's studies? Let's start and stick with stones (i.e., geology), to which I alluded earlier. I remember when I first learned that the Blue Ridge is a result of precisely explainable events like geosynclines, continental collisions, and orogeny. The concept was intellectually exciting; I grasped it immediately; but then suddenly — and, thankfully, only momentarily — the Blue Ridge seemed no longer so beautiful to me. It was as if I were clinically, gynecologically, studying my lover's anatomy. The mystery was gone. At the risk of generalization, I know of no woman who has shared such disappointment in discovering details.

Instead, most women I know can see things in rocks that I could never see. (I almost flunked the field work portion of my college geology course.) They see — and take pleasure in seeing — the textures, consistencies, fissures, shapes and strata, plus colors I don't possess the vocabulary to name. Such eye for detail and the mastery in communicating what is seen escapes me, and most other men I know. I want to learn, and listen intently to women's conversations, but I've come to realize that it's not the content that matters so much as inflections and tones — like a rock's nuanced texture and shade.

And so I have come to doubt that I can ever truly learn all the words that my female narrator would use — and, more important, the way she'd say them. For the language, and thus the knowledge, of women seems still so foreign, as if it's outside the Indo-European family. To me, who can't carry a tune or play a musical instrument, much less stay with the beat in aerobics, it sounds like music. Sometimes, almost a lullaby. Often my most restful sleep comes from nodding off to the background murmur of women's voices — or to the television tuned to some channel like the Home Shopping Network. Hair, makeup, fashion, and the bodies they adorn, talked about in such lovingly endless detail and soothing sounds that the unique meaning of particular words fade into an impressionistic, restful landscape.

When a man tries to impersonate a female, his voice invariably gives him away. It's not simply the baritone or bass (some of the sexiest, most feminine women have low voices). More, it's his lack of animated, gushing sentences, full of glissandos and emphasized syllables and adverbs (as if speaking in italics), and declarative statements that rise like questions, soliciting a listener's attentive connection. When a female impersonator is thus found out, it is said — how appropriately! — that he is "read."

"How did you read me?" a professional impersonator is often heard to ask, so as to be able to improve his performance next time. Like the innocent puzzlement displayed to a respected teacher by a child hungry for knowledge, the question is directed at genuine girls only, the hardest audience to play — never at men, who, when it comes to recognizing textures and shades of meaning, have reading skills seemingly stuck at about the third-grade level.

To them, excited by visual images, appearances are every-thing — and a good-looking female could never ring false.

"I don't know. We could just tell," typically says, usually laughing, the genetic, genuine girl so queried. It's not, alas, the answer — complete with critical analysis and detailed instruction — that the impersonator hoped to hear. But he still can learn, for her laughter and few words speak volumes about the differences that separate him from her. first, there's the intuitive nature of her knowledge — "We could just tell."— about which he can learn only that it can not be learned:

> To be born a woman is to know —
> Although they do not talk of it at school —
> That we must labor to be beautiful.
> — William Butler Yeats, "Adam's Curse"

The next insight revealed by the few words of the impersonator's would-be girlfriend is grounded in the easy transition from "I' to "we" — as in, "I don't know. *We* could just tell." In her first sentence is the feminine ten-dency to shroud the ego: She *does* know, but she refuses to boast about it. (How many men have you ever heard say simply, "I don't know," as she does?) Instead, when she does acknowledge that she knows, she insists on sharing credit with the other real girls around her, who are to-gether joined in laughter.

It is not laughter of derision and ridicule directed at the impersonator; that would be the nervous laughter of men. Rather, the laughter springs from the secret, shared knowl-edge, and resulting emotional intimacy, that seems unique to women. Girlfriends, not the kind that boys have, but girls who are friends with each other, I can only watch their interaction with awed amazement — and pity the poor impersonator who can never have such real girl-friends. Like this would-be woman, I am unable to enter into the confidences of girlfriends or comprehend the mysteries that make their bonds so powerful.

As a man, I can only theorize; and my guesses always touch on that ultimate mystery and beauty of the female body, so mysterious because it's the opposite of mine, so beautiful because only through it can any man be made whole. Like all mysterious beauty, it is vulnerable, and so voluntary self-disclosure becomes a woman's best protec-tion, which in turns allows others like her to share their secrets as well. That's what makes girlfriends, Diana has let me discover. That's the name of my female narrator — Diana. It's her voice that I want to assume. What I think I might know about girls and girlfriends, beyond male-formed stereotypes, I owe to made-up Diana and her imaginary, best girlfriend Stephanie:

I know you want gossip, juicy tidbits, and are just dying to hear bad things — the worse, the better — don't you? But Stephanie is my friend. Really, she is. What's between us is our little secret. I could try to describe her, of course, but I would end up just talking about her wardrobe.

It's fabulous! Tomorrow's always another day with Stephanie, for she never seems to wear the same thing twice. It sounds horrible to say, but friends are really — you've got to admit — just like the clothes we wear. We pick them, we buy them (with money or attention), we match them with our moods, we get comfortable with them, we treasure some, discard others. We like ourselves because of them. Our favorites bring out our personality, the best aspects of which may never before have been revealed. Maybe it's because Stephanie looks so fantastic in aerobics wear, but she reminds me of a black, lycra catsuit. Like Catwoman. Empowered — although Stephanie hates that word, it's so overused, thus unfashionable — is how I feel when I'm with her. It's as if I'd put her skin on. I would never have thought it fit, but it does. Gloriously, as if it were my own. No, not her real skin, silly, but the body-conscious clothes she lets me borrow.

I'm continually amazed at what I learn once I'm inside my female narrator's head (I'll never have her body!). Take the Blue Ridge, for example: The more attentive I become, trying to see as Diana would, as if the landscape were possibly something to wear, the more powerfully mysterious the mountains seem. I'm sure I noticed it before, but I never really saw it before in the thousands of times I've looked — the way the rolling ridges get inversely, progressively darker with distance. The hazy peaks of the Blue Ridge fade into the light blue sky, while the foothills in the foreground are so green, they seem black. The color is not bottle-green, but what is it called exactly? To find just the right word, I have to learn still more. Not simply colors but the fabrics of the land as well, like batiste, brocade, chintz, crinoline, crepe, georgette, organza, taffeta, and tufts of tulle.

To make that observation about the Blue Ridge, then to try to articulate it, as I have just now, I must thank Diana. She makes me conclude what I have long suspected — that until the Piedmont is seen and understood as a feminine landscape, the continually changing and thus forever fashionable kaleidoscope of light and image of the Blue Ridge, whose constant presence on the horizon defines the Piedmont, has little shape or pattern. Diana makes me think — and think things I've never thought before.

To think: What if I really were to become Diana? It would be a change not just of sex but of the whole world around me, turned upside down, a new world in a parallel universe. But why? Would I see things differently simply because I was now a woman, or is it that the world itself would in fact have changed? That is, through the looking-glass of others, I would be seen and treated differently and therefore what I perceive would itself be forced to change? Like the chicken or the egg, biological or cultural determinism, or any inquiry into first causes, this line of questioning reveals, I'm afraid, that I'm still stuck in my male point of view. Endless "why's" are futile, I can hear Diana tell me. The "how" is what matters.

So, yes, if I were a woman, I guess I'd be Diana. I imagine (hope) she's young still, so I'd be a girl, and start all over. The most feminine, seemingly superficial things would captivate me, precisely because a man is normally not allowed to do them. I'd learn how to pluck eyebrows, pamper skin, and paint nails; in finding fun in so doing, I would no longer be the impatient personality I sometimes am. Time and space would take on whole new meanings. I would highlight my hair and experiment with different looks — and, more importantly, talk to my girlfriends about it. They would be the kind of friends, real friends, I'd never had before. I'd still take solitary hikes in the woods, though, and go camping and canoeing, so I might be called a tomboy, but wouldn't mind. I would get in shape, watch my diet, regularly go to aerobics classes but sometimes make excuses not to (e.g. "bad hair day") — and so be in such touch with my own body that its five senses would reveal worlds and universes I'd never known existed in the smallest patch of the Piedmont place that I call home. I would come to know that acceptance of change is not passivity. In trying on the latest fashions — from sweetheart and princess necklines to halter and corset bodices, from mini to maxi, from basque to empire waists, from sheath to A-line, from pleated to sheer — I would be open to transformations, whether magical or simply cosmetic. I'd try all the seemingly infinite colors of lipsticks and eyeshadows, and learn the names by heart. I'd work at whatever works best for me. I would see the land that I love so differently, so incredibly changed that it's like my own new body — and be wiser than I'll ever know. I'd be the most brilliant and accomplished writer ever.

Yes, Diana makes me think — and work. Just like my new best girlfriend Stephanie says. I mean, Diana's best friend. Forever smiling and laughing even when in a sweat and out of breath in aerobics class, Stephanie eggs me onward, in the quest for the Eternal Feminine: "You gotta work it, girl!" &

Das Ewig-Weibliche
Zieht uns hinan.
    — Goethe, concluding lines, *Faust, Part Two*

THE MEANING OF MONEY

DURING a New Year's Eve dinner at the Inn at Little Washington a few years ago, my best friend surprised me — and probably himself— when he rose to make this toast: "I resolve to be worth $50 million by the time I am 50." Our well-bred and socially conscious wives gasped at this display of bad taste or, worse, obscenity — possibly pardoned only by the flowing Dom Perignon that had brought forth a rare boldness in confessing our deepest, formerly most secret, desires. What took me aback, however, was simply the raw content of his dream. He and I had grown up together, shared small-town values, college, and the Army. In the end, was Mammon all there was? Was he not only much richer but also just more honest than I, in finally and candidly recognizing the crass reality of our middle-aged lives?

I never shared any of these thoughts at the time. After all, he was paying for dinner — at surely the most expensive restaurant in Virginia.

Later, equidistant between that New Year and his 50th birthday, the recession-induced collapse of his business meant that he might well lose everything. Instead of creating and building wealth, his energies were consumed in protecting what assets remained from vengefully aggressive bankers. I sometimes gently teased him about his boastful toast, no doubt to distract me from my own "situation."

That's a euphemism for the terror — I can't think of a better word— that then used to grip me at the oddest moments. It hit when I was enjoying my daughter's school concert, when I was in the midst of a business conference call, when I was brushing my teeth, when I was reading fiction of the most escapist kind. And when I was alone in the middle of the night, like T.S. Eliot's "Sweeney Agonistes," I would wake in a sweat and a hell of a fright. I had the hoo-ha's coming to me.

To force the terrible intruder away, I tried to remind myself of all the truly wonderful things for which I was thankful: my family's health, my athletically and academically inclined children, and the generally satisfying professional careers that my wife and I had had. But, instead, I remained consumed by thoughts about money — the money I lost, gone forever in a horrible real estate investment in the Virginia Piedmont countryside.

The beauty of this place into which my money disappeared was no solace. Instead, my experience seemed just another replay in one of the oldest stories on earth: seduced, entrapped, then destroyed by the wiles of beauty. Now, instead of pleasure, I felt pain.

What is it about money lost that is so, well, terrifying? Even though the bottomline is exactly the same, losing money seems so painfully and infinitely worse than not having had it in the first place. Maybe it's the stark and simple difference between despair and hope? Maybe one never knows he had it until he loses it? I don't know the answer, because as a once contented low-roller, I had never before had to confront — and somehow extract

meaning from — a high-stakes investment gone bad.

It seemed like a good idea at the time — so goes the loser's trite lament. The time was three years before the 500th anniversary of Columbus's discovery of the land that made a people rich. The idea was so simple I'd never before explored it: Why not me? Why couldn't I get rich, too, in real estate?

So it was easy to sweet-talk myself into parting with the few liquid assets I had accumulated over the years, to play with the big boys in a once-in-a-lifetime real estate deal. As a tiny partner in a select private investment group, I felt privileged to participate in the purchase of one of the few 18th-Century estates remaining undeveloped amidst the encroaching sprawl of the East Coast's megalopolis. The supply was clearly limited; they just didn't make 500 unspoilt acres, complete with antique-furnished, Georgian manor house, anymore.

Because of this scarcity of supply, I was easily able to construct a veneer of altruism around my basest self-interests — in the best tradition of policy-makers in Big Washington a mere 50 miles away. In buying this grand estate, I told myself, I was helping to preserve the open spaces and heritage of the Piedmont countryside.

The other side of the equation — demand — was where I miscalculated. The burst of the 1980s real estate bubble can be pinpointed, in my microeconomic view, to the precise moment I signed my check for the money I would never see again.

So then I found myself not only throwing good money after bad but also— maybe worse— wasting what could have been productive time in my search for some meaning to help minimize, if not transcend, my loss. Why else would I be spending so many high-risk, low-return hours to write this story?

Recognizing the irony of it all — the Almighty Dollar, which I no longer had, now controlled my life as never before — didn't mitigate the torment: My frayed shirtcollars, my beat-up car, and my maid-less house attested to the fact that I was never an acquisitive kind of guy; but then I found myself desiring things, like a yacht, that I could have bought with the lost money — and I didn't even know how to sail. I had never really played the secretly competitive game of privately computing one's ever growing net worth, as my loose-lipped friend obviously had. Indeed, once when I confided to a boss that money wasn't my primary goal in a job, he dismissed me with the comment, "I've never trusted people who say they're not interested in money." Later, he seemed wiser than I'd ever given credit.

Indeed, all my male friends and professional associates had always talked money, if not in words, certainly in the common currency of actions. Yet seldom had we ever talked *about* money — in the sense of seeking some fundamental understanding that would then have helped explicate my financial loss, so that I could have banished it behind me to get on with my life. For like sex, the importance of money had been simply taken as self-evident; to question its meaning had been unmanly — or just plain stupid. Even to rebel against materialistic excesses, as many of my generation had done in the 1960s, had been simply another way of acknowledging the power of money. A decade later, a once long-haired, unkempt friend would rationalize his metamorphosis into a button-down investment banker by putting it in the context of his student days as a sports star, "Money's just another way of keeping score."

If that was all there is to it, then why did I feel so horrible? I played the game as best I could, and I lost — badly. It was not a tennis game, however; humiliation couldn't be quickly washed away by a post-match shower. What I lost instead was, to the degree that time equals money, a good chunk of my life. Those days, those weeks — indeed, those years — I had worked to earn that money were gone; the deprivations, the small sacrifices, the opportunities not taken, in order to save that same money, now wasted, without meaning. Any illusion of some kind of immortality bestowed by the timeless, inherent worth of one's labors was shattered. So I had to confront my own frailty, even mortality. I moved from denial — let's keep funding the partnership, so the bank note won't go into default — to resignation — let's cut our losses and stoically move on.

Bottomline, I knew that the only peace I could achieve was through understanding. Therefore, I had to accept the fact that I was (a) dumb, (b) victimized, (c) sinful, (d) or some combination of all the above. If the ultimate function of money is to provide a societal framework for rational behavior — to maximize gain, to minimize loss — and I ended up with a big, fat goose egg, then I quite simply had made a wrong choice. QED, I was dumb. If, on the other hand, my choice hadn't been necessarily irrational but simply done in by random events beyond my control (e.g., "the economy"), then painfully I had to forfeit my life-long belief in freewill and forever see myself as a victim . finally, there was an elegant and cleansing simplicity in confessing: I had been greedy! And, so, at the end of the day, sin brought just retribution.

So much for trying to make myself feel better. When it comes to losing money, trying to understand is just another form for regret. The only salvation lies, not in thoughts, but in action: I'll somehow make all the lost money back...and then some. But isn't that what all gamblers say? ❧

Weeks later, one morning, as she was taking a shower, something seemed to slither around her feet. It had to be her imagination. Still, she was afraid to look down. But she felt it again; she looked; and, yes, it was a snake. As she jumped out of the shower, she slammed its sliding, glass door on the snake's head, so hard that blood spewed. The snake wasn't dead, but almost. To put the reptile out of its misery, she ran to the kitchen for a carving knife. The blade was dull. She had to saw and saw. Only after the head finally fell off, with its body still wedged in the noose of the shower door no longer thrashing, did she know it was dead. She never returned to that cottage.

"Poor snake," she would say when recalling the story — never "poor me." Although she never told me so, I know that part of her was pleased that, in at least this one confrontation, the wild things ultimately won, left in control of the battleground after the human adversary retreated. Usually, of course, it's the other way around. We humans seldom make accommodations. If wild creatures get in our way, they die, like road kill. An outcome that now seems rarely in doubt provides for few interesting, much less suspenseful, narratives.

Man against nature — that used to be an exciting and workable theme. But the power of nature is seldom now a force to be reckoned with in most of our daily lives. Even the sometimes violent whims of weather have only occasionally serious, life-or-death consequences for a people who now spend most of their time safely indoors. Nature's revenge in the form of some grand ecological disaster remains, of course, always a distinct possibility — but as a concept only, not felt like fear or awe. To fill this emotional void helps explain perhaps our childlike delight in terror, why young country boys go hunting for poisonous snakes. To want to believe that there remains still something larger than ourselves, which even if we pretend to understand it, we can't control, maybe goes to the heart of our never-satiated fascination with faraway natural disasters like earthquakes and hurricanes, commanding attention disproportionate to their strength and frequency. That's why, I suppose, the so-called 100-year floods that seem to happen every other year or so on the eastern slope of the Blue Ridge attract so many urban gawkers.

With the exception of these truly devastating floods, which not only killed but also suddenly and permanently altered the geography of once peaceful rural communities, the Piedmont of Virginia is a placid place, seductively gentle land. Human intrusions are welcomed, perhaps invited, even solicited. Seldom are these advances resisted, even when they threaten the very sense of time and place that define the place. That is to say, the Piedmont is in no way an Amazon jungle that brings disease and carnivorous creatures to bear on those who would cut it down. Certainly, nowhere can the Piedmont be called a wilderness. And in the sense of being a forbidding and dangerous place for humans, a wilderness it probably never was. The few wild animals that there are seem to be in just the right balance — not the kind or the number to endanger but just enough to fill our need for excitement.

Paradoxically, the closest the Piedmont now comes to wilderness is man-made. Once threatened red-tailed hawks, for instance, perch atop telephone poles on the lookout for easy prey in the Highway Department's freshly mowed killing fields. And when human frustration or laziness allows once cleared forest to become an impenetrable tangle of undergrowth, certain wild animals couldn't ask for a better, safer home.

Deer, for example, thrive in such abandonments, as do their fiercest predators — dogs forsaken by their masters. Packs of these feral canines will run a deer till it drops. Once when I caught sight of such a chase, to even the odds, I lay in wait behind a boulder, a huge stick in hand. As the deer fled past me, white tail flying, I leaped in front of the dogs, waved my stick, and screamed like a banshee. Dogs, it is generally observed, have expressive eyes, and in them I saw the most remarkable combination of shock, puzzlement, and fear. A wild man, they reflected. Such a human, they had never seen before; so, tails between their legs, the dogs ran off in the direction from which they had come — their disregard of the deer complete.

Some Piedmont residents might well wonder what the fuss was all about, since there's already an unnatural abundance of Virginia whitetailed deer (*Odocoileus virginianus*) — in places even more plentiful than when the first English settlers arrived, when Captain John Smith observed, "Of the beastes, the chiefe are Deare." They trample through subdivisions, eat newly planted shrubs down to nubs, and wreck cars when run over. Like cockroaches, they thrive and multiple in environments created by man, who killed off the deer's natural predators. But it is safe to say that most people, even hunters, think of Bambi, not cockroaches, when they see a deer.

The first day of deer season in Virginia falls typically on a Monday, and public schools throughout the state report an unusually high level of truancy that day, as boys are initiated by their fathers through one of America's last remaining rites of passage. That dawn a landowning woman I know awakens after having had an annually recurring nightmare in which she goes hunting for the hunters. Although the dream is filled with blood and guts (she "harvests" three hunters, usually obese with lots of meat) and the woman normally "wouldn't squash an ant," she awakens neither purged nor remorseful but full of hatred toward hunters.

Deer season marks that time of year, probably the only time, when the human population of the Piedmont can be divided into two, neatly defined groups: hunters and nonhunters. But the real division lies in further reductionism: the shrill antihunters and those hunters who, their fellow hunters say, "give all hunters a bad name." The latter shoot just about anything that moves (especially sheep and cows), use flashlights to blind and freeze their targets (called "moonlighting," it's illegal), and shoot from the windows of their cars and pickups after sending dogs into the woods to flush the game toward the road.

As a result, more and more landowners, even those who are avid hunters themselves, now post their land and grant hunting permission to no one but close friends. One Fauquier County farmer's experience is illustrative: After he spotted a circle of buzzards above his fencing along the state road, he discovered a wounded deer left there to die, entangled in barbed wire. By the time he returned with a rifle to end its suffering, it had mercifully expired. He decided to leave the body where it was and to hang a makeshift sign on a nearby tree. With an arrow pointing toward the animal, the sign read: "Dead deer — killed by *brave* hunter." The next day, he found the sign ripped down. So he stood on the top of his truck and nailed the sign farther up the tree trunk, a good 15 feet off the ground. Shortly thereafter the sign was minced with buckshot, illegible.

Like deer, bears are greeted by humans with mixed emotion. Unlike the whitetails, however, there are not many Eastern black bears left, perhaps 2,000 in all of Virginia. In lieu of the real thing, we have placenames: Bear Wallow Road, Bear's Den Farm, Cub Run. So it is that many of us, when we catch a rare glimpse of a real, live bear, feel honored, joyful; we smile or laugh; from a distance, bears seem so cute and cuddly.

They make some people panic, however. "One woman called the state police because she saw a bear and her cubs wandering across a field," recalls an old game warden friend. "When I arrived on the scene, all sorts of people were milling around, and the state police were cruising up and down the road with guns cocked. Crazy people. I told them I'd take them to court if they shot the bears without good cause."

"A black bear is not dangerous unless it has lost its fear of humans and is provoked," says a Game Commission official in Richmond. "That's 99.9 percent true — I'm enough of a biologist to hedge by one-tenth of a percent. But some people act like a bear is a Bengal tiger on the loose, devouring children and mailboxes. The best thing to do if you see a bear is to do nothing, just enjoy watching it, for the bear will leave your subdivision soon enough."

Late autumn is the time of most bear sightings. As the season gets drier, bears enlarge their range tens of miles, and males in particular roam in search of mates. But spring and summer also bring sightings of those few bears, so fearless they seem almost tame, who have come to associate human activity with food. "Picnic-hungry bears," Game officials call them, who hang around like house pets at the dinner table. And like pets, they're often given affectionate names.

Naming may be a kind of taming, but Rambling Rose never did behave; her instincts wouldn't let her. Years ago, this ursine sojourner made all the local papers as the uninvited guest around campfires and picnic tables near the Blue Ridge's Skyline Drive. If the campers and pic-nickers protested, Rambling Rose would insinuate herself with unmannerly tactics of bluff and intimidation. Responding to these reports, Game Commission personnel trapped and relocated her 50 miles away near the West Virginia line. Within five days, there were fresh complaints from Skyline Drive about "a picnic-hungry bear." It was Rambling Rose. This time she was darted with a tranquilizer, since bears are apparently too smart to be live-trapped twice. Again, she was relocated, this time 130 miles away in southwestern Virginia. Within 12 days, a bear with the same modus operandi was reported back on Skyline Drive. On investigation, yes, it was Rambling Rose.

"It's not unusual to see a homing instinct of 35-40 miles among black bears," said a Game Commission research biologist at the time, "but the distance Rambling Rose traveled in so short a period is a record, at least for Virginia. In view of the fact that Rambling Rose was really harmless but with some bad habits and an obvious keen sense of direction, more drastic measures were needed." So in August of that year, the bear was relocated to the Great Dismal Swamp. Not only the distance (200 air miles away) but also the different terrain and prime habitat would overcome the bear's homing instinct. Or so it was thought. A month later, Rambling Rose was hit by a car and killed — on her way home.

My own Rambling Rose story has a happier ending and is much closer to home — both mine and the possum's. A few springs ago, a tree surgeon convinced me that one of the towering, old sycamores lining the driveway should be cut down. Some limbs were rotting, the trunk was hollow, and it was leaning precipitously. It could fall anytime, this tree expert told me, and hit somebody, who then would sue me. By the time he and his crew had done their deed, the bill had climbed as high as some legal fees, not to mention the cost to other, healthy trees that the supposed expert arborist damaged in the felling. I never told my mother, whose property it had once been, and hoped that she would never notice. Her way was always to let nature take care of itself. Of course, on her very next visit, not long before she died, she immediately remarked upon the bare spot where the tree had once been.

Meanwhile, the family dog began acting strangely. A combination beagle and terrier, she used to sit by the door just waiting for the chance to explore outdoors and escape the bonds of domesticity; once outside, it took tricks and bribes to lure her back in. But now it was as if the house had been suddenly transformed into a home entertainment center for dogs, as she just lay happily in the corner of the living room, wagging her tail, when she wasn't sniffing between the cracks of the random-width floorboards. Sometimes she barked and growled at whatever it was she was smelling. And sometimes she scratched; fleas began appearing from nowhere.

The mystery was solved one morning when I heard my wife scream from the basement, where she had gone to do some laundry. The scream was not so much of terror but of recognition; she had come face to face with North America's only native marsupial, which in the words of Captain John Smith's first description, "hath an head like a Swine, and a taile like a Rat, and is the bigness of a Cat."

The possum and its family that used to live in the hollowed out sycamore had taken up residence in the basement under our living room. The space between the joists and stone foundation made a fine home. At first, my wife insisted that we somehow get rid of the possum family. "Somehow" was a euphemism for painfully dislocating the poor possums again or killing them out right, I told her. I pointed out that the dog had never been more content, that the exciting presence of possums was converting our still somewhat savage pet into a true house dog. Then, I surprised even myself when I began to sing, "People who need wild things are the luckiest ..." to the off-key tune of her favorite Barbra Streisand song.

And, yes, now that we've got the fleas under control, we're all one big happy family — the possums, the dog, my wife, our new baby, my daughters when they're home from school, and me. I know that my mother, now dead, would bless us. ❧

GHOSTS

LIKE most Virginians, I grew up on ghost stories. They were told after dinner and before bedtime by adults whose voices were quiet and serious and therefore wise. Now that I think about it, these voices themselves sounded ghost-like, disembodied; for as I listened, my eyes were seldom directed at the speaker — but, instead, out the window into the dark unknown or into the fireplace's burning coals, where an imagination doesn't have to be lively to conjure up just about any shape there is or isn't, worldly or otherwise.

Though terrified, curiously I was never afraid. It must have been a child's delight in terror. And to the degree that we remain child-like, the supernatural not only continues to intrigue but also very much seems a real possibility. And so to this day, I remember the stories. Such lasting power must make them, at least on some level, true. And those voices, although the same ones that spoke of Santa Claus, they would never lie. I believed.

My stepfather believed, surely he did. It was in his voice, as he recounted the stories. And I never knew Randy to lie, not once about anything. Or if he wasn't totally certain in his belief (he never actually saw a ghost himself), he wanted to believe. As if to create a foundation for this faith, Randy approached the phenomena of ghosts with scientific curiosity and rigor (he was by profession an engineer). Over the years, he had collected thick files of ghost stories, containing scrupulously transcribed, firsthand accounts. If the person relating the story to him wasn't an actual eyewitness, but only an acquaintance of someone who had purportedly seen a ghost, Randy didn't bother recording the tale. Born around the turn of the century, he had used this same method, in his travels around the Piedmont, to record first-hand accounts of both Civil War veterans and former slaves.

But he didn't need the stacks of files he'd accumulated to repeat the ghost stories; all these Randy knew by heart. In the telling, his was not the animated voice of an evangelist, but of a respectful son of the Piedmont speaking reverently of those who had shared its same earth before him. His quiet, uninflected way of speaking forced a listener to attentiveness. My mind's eye can still see him, sitting as usual in the armchair next to the fireplace, pipe in hand, as we in the room begged him to tell one of his stories — and then another. Even as I became older, more interested in the here-and-now of adolescent girls than anything as remote as a presence from the past, I soon found that sharing one of Randy's many ghost stories was a sure way to break any awkward, first-date silences. Although my story-telling techniques never approached the quality of Randy's, they served my immediate purposes at the time.

Here's one of my favorites. It's as if I can hear my stepfather talking:

"It was back in the early Thirties. Two members of the local school board were taking a drive out Old Waterloo Road. Brand new car, a Ford, I think. The driver, Lewellyn, was showing off, taking his friend for a drive. Middle of the day, sun bright and shining, not a cloud in the sky. But in those days they were just about the only car on the road.

"All of a sudden, for no reason, the car stopped. Just stopped, on a curve and slight rise in the road. I can show you the spot today. You probably know exactly where I'm talking about. About three miles out of town, as the road dips and starts up again after that long, twisty downhill stretch. A stream and woods are on the left, and an old stone wall and pasture are on the right. The small bridge over the stream, as the road cuts over it, is just up ahead a couple of hundred yards.

"Anyway, the car just stops, dead. And Lewellyn sees in front of him a group of men straggling out of the woods. They're dirty and exhausted, dragging gear and rifles. Some of the men are so weak, they have to be helped and supported by others. The funny thing is, he realizes that the men are dressed in clothes so old they look like they're from another century. And the rifles aren't like any he's ever used; they're more like muskets. And one of the men is carrying some kind of banner or battle flag. They must be soldiers, but they look like ragamuffins. Then, when they get to the other side of the road, they climb over the stone wall and just disappear. Like they were never there. There's not a single soul to be seen anywhere in the field.

"Lewellyn, who I knew to be a very matter-of-fact man — he ran the big supply store up on Main Street and was picked chairman of the school board — he, of course, just assumed he'd blacked out or something, and didn't dare tell his traveling companion what he'd just seen. Or thought he'd seen. So he started the car back up, and headed on down the road through the spot where the soldiers had just crossed, as if nothing had happened.

"After driving a while, he noticed that his companion, normally a gregarious sort, wasn't talking at all. Totally silent. So he looked over at him, and he was white as a sheet. 'Tom,' he said, 'what's a matter?' At first, Tom was reluctant to say anything, he was afraid that Lewellyn would think he was crazy. But, then, after Lewellyn kept asking him what was wrong, he proceeded to describe the exact same scene that Lewellyn had witnessed. Bedraggled soldiers from another time."

That exchange between Lewellyn and Tom was, to Randy, the key to the story, made it real and true, as if he were a detective with two, independent eyewitnesses each confirming exactly what the other had seen. That neither Lewellyn nor Tom was frightened by what they'd witnessed also verified their account, according to Randy.

"Awe" was what they said they felt. And this was the most common reaction, Randy found in all his research, of those people who claimed to have been visited by any kind of ghostly apparition. Fear, they never felt. If people were afraid, what they saw must have come from within themselves, a production of imagination.

Later, on reflection, the initial awe that a true ghost sighting inspired was transfigured into a sense of being privileged, honored, even blessed. That, at least, is what the ghost-sighters said, without exception. And Randy made pilgrimages throughout Virginia to the sites of reported ghost sightings not only to talk to witnesses but also, I think, in the hope that he might be blessed as well. It never happened. No matter how much he believed or wanted to believe, it never happened. He could have lied, but he didn't.

The closest encounter he ever had was as a young man on a horse. Growing up on his family's farm, he regularly rode his horse to school. As he returned by the usual path one afternoon, near an old mill called Auburn, the horse suddenly halted and, despite numerous kicks to the ribs and a whip on the rear, refused to go forward. The place, a small ravine carved by a stream, was as familiar as the home stable to the horse, having passed that way without incident a thousand times or better — and would at least a thousand more. But that afternoon there was something strange about the place, so strange that the horse stopped still — no, not still, he shook. The tremors from the horse shot up Randy's legs and made his body shiver But he wasn't afraid.

He dismounted, held the reins, and looked around. There was no evidence of a wild animal or anything else that could have spooked the horse. Anything real, that is. The paranormal was another matter. Still quavering, the skittish horse had to be led to the other side of the stream, where Randy remounted and rode on home as if nothing had ever happened.

Over the years, as he grew older, Randy returned often to that same spot, hoping to duplicate the experience, somehow to see what the horse had sensed. It never happened; but, quite independently, while doing historical research, Randy did learn that it was here, this very place, where a young Confederate, under the command of John Singleton Mosby (the so-called "Gray Ghost"), had been shot from his horse and killed. By all accounts, Randy's great-uncle, Nick Carter, who also rode with Mosby's Rangers, had been there, too, a witness to his good friend's death.

That Randy, before he died, never himself got to behold this young Confederate horseman, or any other ghost, did not weaken, but only tested, Randy's faith. I, too, have never seen a ghost; but, unlike Randy, I do not profess or pretend to believe. At best, I'm an agnostic. Still, I must confess that while I write this, in the 18th-Century house where Randy once lived, I'm acutely aware of creaking floorboards, knocking pipes, sudden drafts of cold air, and any other sensation of unexplained origins. In the attic, an unnailed, handhewn rafter every so often appears to move miraculously, and the rich aroma of country ham sometimes seems to waft from the porch, where the old kitchen used to be. And, yes, in the library, where Randy once sat and told his ghost stories, I occasionally think I can smell his pipe.

What else should I expect from a 200-year-old, clapboard house? For history and ghosts are inseparable. One is the built and recorded past; the other, the past revealed — through not simply dry wood or dry words, but a "living" presence. Maybe there's even a logical explanation for such ghostly physicalities: Since matter is never created or destroyed, as Randy the mechanical engineer knew well, isn't it possible that remnants of bodily energy always remain? But, when it comes to spirits, explanations are not necessarily needed or even desirable. Even if I can't truthfully say myself that I accept the possibility, much less the existence, of ghosts, the fact that others believe, as Randy believed, is enough to make one feel the power and the presence of the past — and of something more, perhaps.

Perhaps. ❧

At Home in Foreign Waters

THE seasons pass seamlessly in the landlocked Piedmont. Only when spring or summer is long gone, and it is therefore missed, are you aware that the earth is moving in orbit around the sun. No ticks, tocks, alarms, or rush hours — only residual agricultural rhythms of planting and harvesting — to mark the passage of time in the Piedmont. Instead, time blends here in a subtle mixture of memory and anticipation: hints of what's to come, a gentle foreshadowing, like an unusually cool, clear August night, with some of the leaves that rustle not so richly green anymore; or a brazen reminder, like an 80-degree day in the dead of winter.

It's a fluid calendar that I've grown used to.

Summer ends, not with the autumnal equinox or Labor Day, but with the last swim. It used to be a final leap into what was left after a dry spell of the old swimming hole, its tepid and shallow water mirroring my own sadness that school would begin tomorrow. With age and adulthood's search for ever bigger waters, if not greener pastures, the ritual has been refined on the rocky coast of Maine, whose only visible connection with the Piedmont are the ubiquitous Civil-War-era memorials and gravestones inscribed "died in Virginia."

My family's vacation cottage is locked and shuttered; the car is packed, ready to head south, except for the towels and bathing suits hanging on the wobbly porch railing. We time our departure to high tide, when the Maine waters are warmed, ever so slightly, by the rocks that had recently baked in the sun.

What's become almost a liturgy is this: We climb along the jagged shoreline to the place where it is deep enough to dive. Knowing it is the last time this year or maybe even forever — I've reached the age where the phrase "next summer" might be wishful thinking — makes each slippery-with-seaweed step fixed in memory.

I know I will always remember our family's individual personalities as revealed in how we address Casco Bay. It's important to my older daughter to be the first one in, with a whoop and a dive, gracefully cutting the water near a lobster pot. My younger daughter prefers the gradualist approach, with soft gasps punctuating her incremental submersion into the chilly waters. My wife, arms flailing; jumps and lets out a controlled alto shriek, as if an opera diva. As for me, I'm never quite sure what my body will do; it depends on my level of courage at that precise moment. We each approach water, I realize, as we live life; sometimes tentatively, timidly, yet savoring each moment; at other times with all deliberate speed, a rush to seize and take control of time, to get it over with, to make time present into time past, as quickly as possible. And I must confess that as I get older and more sensitive to the cold, I think I enjoy the memory more than the moment.

But I still cannot resist the water, whose sirens and naiads beckon wherever I travel. While others may revel in meals and museums, I cherish the oceans and lakes — and the rivers and streams that feed them. They keep me

young. Or at least the impulse they inspire seems youthful, even adolescent:

The urge is to leap into unknown waters just to say you'd done it.

Thus, though I can't really say I ever swam the English Channel, I've stuck my toes in — bilingually, as it were, on both sides, long before there was a Chunnel. And once, on a long-ago birthday, while my girlfriend took the high road, I took the plunge off the bonny shores into Loch Lomond. Sipping a new white wine while floating in a blue Danube brook is my tale from the Vienna Woods.

Back in the United States, to keep myself awake on the monotonous macadam of my one cross-country trip meant not coffee breaks but dips in the Great Lakes (almost each and every one), the Wisconsin Dells, Mississippi headwaters, the Platte and the wide Missouri, the Columbia and the Snake. Visiting friends in Nantucket, I had to sample what felt like primordial soup beyond Coatue Point, at the shallow Head of the Harbor, where the scallops lived that we ate. My first long goodbye to my daughters — at summer camp in the Great Smokies — prompted a belly-flop into the nearby Chattooga, the river of James Dickey's *Deliverance*, for my own deliverance from the tears I didn't show.

I don't need the River Lethe. To cause forgetfulness when work and the world are too much with me, any old, unnamed pond will do. For the surest escape from the bonds of terra firma must by definition be liquid, and if travel means to see, to explore, then not to lunge head first into the world's waters is equivalent to being buried deep in the soil as a couch potato. A travel destination without water to swim in, to me, is no vacation at all. In dry lands, in dry seasons, a natatorium will suffice. Daily in a Northern Virginia health club's lap pool, I stroke toward my next vacation. Actually, I'm already there, for swimming frees the mind to travel. I could be anywhere. Except for the chlorine and the absence of saline buoyancy, it could be the Caribbean. Through my blurred racer's goggles, as if snorkeling the reefs, I can see a phantasm of brain coral, angelfish, damselfish, sea stars, and lavender tube sponge. Or, with eyes closed, my cupped hand hits the lane-divider rope, and it could be a crab pot in the Chesapeake Bay. Or, back in the pool, I imagine that Jamaican resort called Ciboney, whose promotional ads proclaim 90 swimming pools, a different one for every villa.

So it is that, while swimming laps, the thought occurs: I could swim around the world. I'm reminded of John Cheever's classic short story "The Swimmer." If that tale's suburban Odysseus could make it all the way home by swimming his neighbors' backyard pools, then, yes, it's possible, I could — before I die — swim around the world. Not literally, of course; for then I would surely, quickly die. But just to entertain the obvious dangers, as with all truly excellent travel adventures, is exhilarating: negotiating the rocks where the North Atlantic meets the Hebrides, navigating the busy shipping lanes of the Hellespont, playing cat and mouse with sharks in the Coral Sea off Australia, being swept along by mountainous tidal waves over the Pacific deep, or, for a freshwater break, letting my body cascade over Victoria Falls.   At a slow but steady breast stroke pace, I calculate, it would take three to four years to circumnavigate the globe. But allowing for headwinds and crosscurrents, sleep and food, as well as periodic treatments for hypothermia and pollution poisoning, I must prudently figure more like eight years. That's quite a lengthy sabbatical—and who would be crazy enough to be cajoled into sailing the companion boat necessary for my rest, recuperation, and inevitable rescue?

So it must remain forever just another one of those impossible dream vacations. Simply to test the waters, in my travels wherever I go, must be contentment enough. While my daughters collect polished glass on the rocky Maine coast, seashells at Sanibel, and ghost stories at Pawleys Island, I swim. Water may be universal, but it is always different: Simply the way the angle of the sunlight plays on the surface, from clear azure pools to heavy gray swells, is unique to that one spot on earth. And, as Heraclitus knew, you can't step into even the same river twice. But the names attached to unique bodies of waters are changeless. They always entice. To say the name, then to swim what's named, is to make that body yours. Like Menemsha Pond and Squibnocket Bight on Martha's Vineyard.

I can still remember floating on my back off Squibnocket Point, looking into the liquid sky, and thinking: I'm home. The waters were foreign—I had never before been to Martha's Vineyard — yet so familiar. Enveloped within their gentle waves, I was an island too, and could feel the earth move — a fluid planet.

As the sun began to set, the horizon's haze seemed to steam and sizzle. A gull, blinded by the sun on my exact same plane, didn't see me and almost landed on my nose. To be at one with the sea means, even for an aging swimmer, to be reborn. No wonder, then, that rites — of baptism, christening, initiating, naming — require water. For that's where life began, the sea. I learned that fact long ago at school, but true knowledge comes only while immersed. Only when you feel it—the water—do you know for sure. Who really feels the air? Breathing is so routine, typically taken for granted. To get away from it all—if that's what a real vacation is — must surely mean leaving one's element behind, trading air for water. And death for time. ❧

Beauty and Death (The View From Ashby's Gap)

I wonder how many people died watching the O. J. Simpson trial. Dosing in and out of morphine-clouded consciousness in hospice wards across the country, they watched, prone but for pillow-propped heads, eyes lidded yet uplifted, peering from elevated hospital beds toward the television sets mounted on metal brackets high, near the ceiling, on otherwise undecorated, stark white walls. As for my mother, she seemed to prefer the Weather Channel.

But first, because it's easier, I must come to terms with another death, the death of someone I never even met, about whose life I know absolutely nothing. Only in death is there some kind of knowledge, a bond informed with meaning, a felt connection; it seems almost like a blood tie, this curious nexus, both terrible and somehow beautiful. Yes, this has to do with beauty, I think — with what we want to see, what pleases us, and the truth we think we know.

It started out not on CNN but as a three-inch story buried on page A14 of my hometown weekly that, among all my other supposed required reading, usually lies forgotten at the bottom of the stratified paper pile. Why that week, like a diligent geologist, I dug out the newspaper, much less got as far as the inside pages, I can't tell you; but the small (hardly bigger than the type on this page) headline caught my eye: "Man Dies In Paris Car Wreck."

No, not *Paris*, but Paris, Virginia; still, there's a tenuous tie — the tiny Piedmont village was named in 1819 in honor of the French home of the Marquis de Lafayette, American Revolutionary War hero. And it remains today, in the unspoilt heart of Virginia hunt country, much as it was then — a cozy cluster of 19th-Century log, clapboard, and brick buildings nestled amid rocky yet fertile farmland hard on the eastern slope of the Blue Ridge. "As charming a spot as in the world," recently conceded a visiting French friend — but only after first teasing me about the town's grandiose appellation.

About the man who was killed on the outskirts of Paris, Virginia, all that I know is what most of us nowadays know about most things: what we learn from the news. Here's what I read in the newspaper: He lived in the Washington, D.C. suburbs, some 30 miles away. His age was 62. His car, a 1992 Ford Thunderbird, which was the only vehicle involved in the wreck, incurred approximately $8,000 in damages. Traveling east on Route 50, the car ran off the road, went airborne, then struck a guard rail. The occupant was wearing his seat belt at the time of the accident, and there was no evidence that speeding or alcohol was involved, according to the State Police. Their investigation was continuing.

That was it, end of story, the extent of the media coverage. It reminded me of the kind of on-deadline piece I would have filed 30 years ago as a cub reporter on a similar small town weekly. All the known facts — and to be a fact, it had to be epistemologically attributed to an objective and therefore higher authority than the reporter

himself, like police or witnesses — were compressed or expanded, like subjective time, into whatever space was available. "Endit" or "-30-," I was taught to type at the bottom of the last page of copy. And normally that would indeed have been the end of the story. Quickly forgotten by readers, even eventually by the writer, the news hole became a black hole.

But later, as a wire service reporter, I would learn to resurrect a dead story into news again for client newspapers with different deadlines. (Our motto at United Press International: "A Deadline Every Minute.") The easiest method was simply to transform a buried sentence into a lead, with the body of the story unchanged. For example, "A man was killed in Paris, Virginia, yesterday when his car...." might be the lead for morning papers, then recycled for the p.m. papers into: "Police today continued their investigation into the Paris auto accident that claimed a man's life...." But, depending upon the celebrity quotient of the victim, that kind of rewriting could last through only a limited number of news cycles. Commonplace auto fatalities, no matter how inexplicable the circumstances, simply aren't the stuff of running stories.

So why does this single, small newspaper story fascinate, even haunt, me still? Though a true story, never was it truly a story at all in the sense of "news that stays news." That's the way Ezra Pound defined literature, stories that last. Yet also fascinating — and frustrating — is how the truth of any story can be buried, lost entirely, in too much information. Story? What story? This particular newspaper story was simply a recitation of known, not necessarily connected, facts. It was up to me, as it is you, any reader, to fashion truth and meaning. To fathom death, to try to understand it, we need to tell and hear stories, to establish meaning where there seemed none. Even random deaths. As it stood, this was no story at all — but, rather, simply the reporting of an event; death is but an event, particularly an unnatural death, that all newspapers of record must report.

At best, it was an "unsolved mystery" as in the syndicated television series by that name. Lots of suspicions and dead-end leads in a thin narrative thread. But no way — not yet anyway — could it merit being called a true mystery in the literary sense, for it lacked the character development, motive, plotting, and conflict of that genre. In what was omitted, however, was a clue, the suggestion of something more. A tiny fact mentioned in passing, dangling with possible meaning, then dropped with no explanation, no context. It appeared in one sentence only, but gave my imagination something to hold onto, perhaps even to attach meaning to, and to create mystery. I read it again. And again:

"Witnesses at the scene told police that the victim had been holding a video camera in one hand when the accident occurred."

Ashby's Gap, that's the name where the road there at Paris cuts through the mountains. Of all the thoroughfares across the Blue Ridge, it is perhaps the gentlest, certainly the least elevated (only 1,100 feet above sea level), yet it commands as breathtaking views as any of the more rugged and steeper mountain passes with names like Thornton, Rockfish, and Swift Run Gaps. To the west, one's gaze sweeps down over the great Valley of Virginia, drained by the Shenandoah, unfolding northward toward historic Harper's Ferry and the river's confluence with the Potomac, where the view, Thomas Jefferson wrote, was "worth a trip across the Atlantic."

But it is the view from the east side of Ashby's Gap, its Piedmont vista, that interests me, as it apparently did the man whose car crashed here. Upon cresting the ridge and encountering the rolling panorama of the Piedmont, one beholds a view that makes it hard to keep one's eyes on the road. To come upon this view for the first time, unexpectedly — the gradual incline, with very few twists and turns, leaves a driver totally unprepared — is like a revelation.

This is not the road to Damascus, however; the Virginia town of that name is many miles away, in the southwestern corner of the state. Nor is it really the road to Paris anymore, for the new, dual-lane Route 50 skirts the village, by a hundred yards or so, as cars and trucks whiz by at 65 miles per hour to and from the Northern Virginia suburbs. And it is here that the man I know only from the newspaper story lost his life.

I traveled that road repeatedly, back and forth across the

mountains, from the Virginia Piedmont, where my mother was born and lived most of her life, to the West Virginia Panhandle, where she lay dying. On the borderline between geographic regions and between life and death. We didn't know she was dying, not for sure, not even the doctors, who were continually confounded by her body's doing the unexpected. The one day they thought she'd die, she didn't. From then on (she lived another six weeks), the doctors never made another prediction.

"You shouldn't have come," she would always chastise me, her face in mock anger, during those first weeks in the hospital. "It's such a long ways." Her voice would soften, so I would know that she knew that I knew she was pleased I'd made the trip. "But it's so pretty," I'd say, "particularly pretty, the view from Ashby's Gap today." I'd then describe in detail what she already knew by heart, paint the picture with an appreciation I'd learned from her. There's something soothing in retold stories, where what happens next is always known. There's a comforting lack of suspense — that necessary emotional ingredient for mystery — in the view from Ashby's Gap. Even when the fields are parched from drought, as they were that summer, to see them and then to say what was seen brings pleasure. The pleasure of peace. "Restful and peaceful," those in fact were the words I usually used to describe the view, as I did that morning, with her husband of 20 years, Nathan, at her bedside too.

"You'll be there soon. You'll be home soon," he said, for he was tired from her night of pain. "It'll be so restful and peaceful." He turned his head and cried. And that was the closest anybody came to talking about death: At rest, at peace, tranquility, home at last. The land on the other side of the mountains, the Piedmont, that she had always called home was so restful, so peaceful, so tranquil.

Driving back and forth across the mountains between the Piedmont and the Panhandle almost daily that summer, I would often play with the words and wonder: Why do these particular adjectives — restful, peaceful — describe the feelings inspired by a beautiful landscape? But are they feelings at all? Rather, perhaps, the absence of feeling? The wilting away of emotion? Is that what sublimity is? Why, then, do most definitions of art, which often aspires to such landscape-like beauty, invoke emotion evoked?

Anytime I need a hit of emotion, however, I don't need to commit myself to anything as grand as an art gallery visit — but simply flip my car radio to the nearest and clearest "Oldies-but-Goodies" station. Nostalgia, it's easy to dismiss; but surely if feelings are the measure of meaning, then those of my adolescence, when rock-and-roll was young, seem the most intensely felt, what formed this 50-year-old man I have now become.

That summer I drove with radio off, but I could still hear music. The refrains were in the passing landscape. Usually it's the other way around: To hear something, even to taste or smell something, Proust-like, is to inspire images; but the visual — I wonder why — seldom invites intrusions from other senses' memories. Eyes only — "I see" means "I understand." To hear Brahms is to visualize an autumn woods perhaps; but I've known only one person who could do the opposite. He couldn't help hearing Mozart allegros, he said, as we walked the waving meadows of Virginia's Piedmont one brilliant spring day. An Italian, from its own Piedmont region in fact, he and I had worked briefly together in Washington before he returned to Europe. The last I heard of him, he had suffered a nervous breakdown and was in a sanatorium somewhere in Switzerland. So now I think of Thomas Mann's *The Magic Mountain* whenever I hear the same music he heard in the shadow of the Blue Ridge. What convoluted, complex connections human consciousness, like mine, spins before it vanishes in death.

But now it was not Mozart or Brahms that I heard that summer; instead, the radio-less silence was filled with Gregorian chants. Not the sounds themselves, try as I might to imagine them as I crossed Ashby's Gap, but thoughts of Gregorian chants. That was the only music my mother had asked that I bring to play in her hospital room. No Glenn Miller or other Big Band sounds from her own youth, her own oldies but goodies. "Those monks singing," is all she had answered when I had asked if I could bring her something special to play on the CD-player I had brought already. What she had asked for, these chants, are not really music at all: no beat, no

passage of time, no temporal or emotional change at all except pitch and timbre, resonating like the weather and seasons in the richly tonal, limitless landscape as viewed from Ashby's Gap.

Tranquil, peaceful, restful, so restful.... So beautiful. But so presumably is death, restful and peaceful. Are they both, then, somehow the same, beauty and death? To ponder beauty, it occurred to me driving back across the mountains, is always easier than to think about death. Easier, still, not to have thought at all. To think even tiny thoughts was to worry that the change-of-shift nurses would not know how to work the CD-player and, in my absence, my mother would have only the silence of her own thoughts. To think is to know that we all must die. But the absence of thought, that's even worse, for that's what death is, isn't it? I no longer think, therefore I'm not.

The problem with driving a car is that, like watching television (even a supposedly suspenseful murder trial), it requires very little thought. It's almost a reflex act: an automatic response to a stimulus that involves a nerve impulse passing inward from a receptor (e.g., the eye) to a nerve center and thence outward to an effector (like the muscle of the hand holding the steering wheel) without reaching the level of consciousness. So the driver/viewer's unoccupied mind turns to other things — not thinking about driving or watching the road (and its peripheral sights) but thinking about thinking and watching one's self watch. So it was that, while driving through Ashby's

Gap, I no longer so much experienced beauty as pondered why it's beautiful. Such self-consciousness was not unlike my wife's catching me staring at a pretty girl, whom I wasn't even aware I was staring at until I was caught. Similarly, I often used to find my head turning involuntarily from the road ahead of me, where I was going, where I should be looking, to the side, pulled, eyes drawn, to expanses beyond, whether open water like the Potomac along the George Washington Parkway, or a wide panorama like that at Ashby's Gap. I hadn't even known I was looking until I suddenly caught myself swerving off the road and crashing into the very same trees that had provided foreground and perspective to the view that had captivated me so.

Not wanting to think anymore, I turned the car's radio on to NPR and listened to other people's thoughts, their attempts at least to shape them into words. I'm not one of those listeners who talk back to the radio. Information is simply absorbed, like pop music lyrics. The words flow in, the words flow out, emptying my mind of any personal memory or meaning. So restful, so peaceful:

I felt myself falling asleep at the wheel. I realized I had better stop for a cup of coffee before I crossed the Shenandoah. On the other side of the river there would be no place to stop. The sky was dark already, and the mountain my car had to climb was darker still. Once on the top of Paris Mountain, I could look down on the other side and see the consoling lights of domestic tranquility, the windows of isolated farmhouses illuminated, dotting the landscape like stars. So restful, so peaceful, the scene and the people I imagined in it.

It is the human presence, the figure in the landscape, that has provided the subject for most art, man's attempt to create beauty. Is that why the view from Ashby's Gap is considered so beautiful? The distance is such that no people can be seen, but their presence is surely felt. Would it still be beautiful if the forest had never been cleared to demonstrate human primacy, stone and split-rail fences never erected to convey control and ownership, fields never cultivated to elicit contrasting shades of green and brown, homesteads never built in what once was wilderness to suggest man's harmony with nature?

Certainly, such a scene would have generated little interest for the Late Gothic miniaturists and Renaissance masters, whose landscapes provided background only to the time and space occupied by humans on this earth. To try to capture pure, natural landscapes is a relatively new impulse, and such painting did not become popular until the Nineteenth Century. In America, it was closest painting ever came to religious art. So, in the Age of Industrialization, did these — often spiritual, always idealized — landscape paintings simply represent a newfound appreciation for what was being lost? For the first time, maybe, one could really "see" the view.

Pragmatically, that's the case at Ashby's Gap. No dense forest or other vestige of wilderness blocks the view, and a dual-line highway makes the view easily accessible. But there are no scenic overlooks on which to park the car and ponder. It's only a fleeting glimpse that a car traveling at 65-miles-per-hour can offer. And so it was, I theorize, that the man who was killed on Ashby's Gap tried to "save" the beauty here for further viewing — on his VCR at home. Videotape was his canvas.

The only problem with my hypothesis was that the canvas was blank, according to the State Trooper who had investigated the accident. As if I still worked as a reporter, I had felt compelled to call the police, to find out more about this accident that obsessed me. And like most reporters, I already had the lead written in my mind; all I needed were a few facts to fill in my preconceived story line. Yes, the Trooper said, my theory about why the car ran off the road made sense, and one of the very first things he had done was to view the tape that had been in the camera clasped in the accident victim's hand. But, no, there was nothing on the tape, it was absolutely blank. So much for my attempt to make sense of things, to shape the dust of facts into a recognizable shape like a mountain, to provide meaning where there was none, to fill my need to find an easy explanation for death.

The Trooper must have detected my disappointment. "That doesn't mean you're not right," he said. "Maybe the fellow was trying to get his camera to record the view when his car ran off the road, and that's why the tape was blank. We'll never know."

In the interest of knowing, let's assume for the moment that the tape was not blank — but, instead, had actually recorded what he had last seen, this ideal of beauty for which he may well have laid down his life. What would I have hoped to see? A swirling montage, a new kind of impressionism, of a landscape that would inspire the artist in all of us? Or, more sensationally, some kind of snuff film? "Beauty to Die For," that could have been the video's title. Maybe it could even have made the local TV Action News, if not CNN. "Virginia man sacrifices self for beauty," would have intoned perhaps the pretty/handsome anchorperson, setting up the film clip. What would viewers, the well-informed citizenry, then see?

A solitary tree, a chestnut oak perhaps, appears to move, jerkily up and down and sideways, finally swirling. The angle of vision, too tight, now widens; the tree becomes the foreground's focal point; but the eye is now pulled beyond bark and limbs, swept to the horizon. Between the tree and the horizon the viewer's imagination instantly fills in the blanks. Shades of green roll, like the agitated water; specks of white, which must be houses and out-buildings but could just as well be ships and their lifeboats. Then, suddenly, the viewer feels seasick as the camera rolls, first blue skyward, circling the heavens, then down-ward to a glimpse of what must be a guardrail. The camera lens — or is it the windshield? — splinters. Then, the dashboard and darkness, as a voice can be heard, almost drowned by the metallic crashing: "Oh, God."

In the best, even the most representational, art, there is abstraction, a transcendence from the particular to something more. The view from Ashby's Gap provides one particular scene, but the pure form of it, the Platonic idea of it, is what the rolling hills of the Virginia Piedmont are all about. The scene is picture-perfect already; so no great painters that I know of have ever even tried to capture it; they would risk sentimentality; the picture would be too idealized. The contours of the land are too perfectly curved; the solitary farmhouses, too cozy; the meandering dirt and gravel roads connecting them, too affected in their pleasing arcs, as if built for pleasure only, with no realistic purpose or linear efficiency in mind; man's relationship with nature, too harmonious, as fences detour around streams and outbuildings are camouflaged by trees left standing. Or for the writer attempting to describe the scene, it just wouldn't make good copy; there's no conflict; the only drama, weather.

"That's as pretty as a (expletive deleted) picture," I can easily imagine many an unsuspecting and surprised motorist uttering when suddenly encountering the view from Ashby's Gap for the first time. I know those were the words I was shocked to hear coming from the agape mouth of the most street-wise punk I've ever met when he saw his very first rural sunrise. The scene was not Ashby's Gap, but a Carolina boot camp 30 years ago; we were both U. S. Army recruits, a newly graduated college kid from Virginia and a high school dropout from the sunless canyons of a New York City ghetto, standing side by side for our first reveille. That there was anyone alive who had not seen a sunrise was shock enough for a country boy like me. That the perception of beauty must be universal, that appreciation doesn't just come from learning, was a real education for a smart-aleck like me. But mostly I was shocked that his reaction was so genuine and spontaneous, he couldn't hide it behind the tough-guy persona he'd groomed. Only the expletive he added to "picture" preserved his tough self-image.

What is it exactly about a sunrise, a sunset, or the view from Ashby's Gap? Why are they beautiful? So beautiful, they make us stop and stare. We're amazed that they mirror so exactly our mental images, so fulfill our expectations, like leitmotifs or variations on a familiar theme in the greatest music. So beautiful, perhaps too beautiful, so perfectly matching pictures already existing in our heads that our critical faculties dismiss what we see as overused, trite, and, yes, picturesque; but even then, the emotion that their beauty evokes can not be denied.

So is beauty objectively intrinsic to what is beautiful, or simply defined by the emotional nature of our response? Truly universal, or culturally derived — does the view from Ashby's Gap awe, for instance, only those schooled in American heritage? Is the expression of beauty, and its appreciation, a moral virtue — and so the well-trimmed fences, the man-made ponds, the freshly hayed fields at Ashby's Gap earn our restful contemplation of labor well done? And the gentle Piedmont creates gentlemanly behavior, while an ugly environment, like a blighted inner city, leads to evil acts? And so does it follow that if the man-molded landscape like that at Paris, Virginia, shows what freewill can accomplish when we're good, then is this landscape's beauty enough justification to deprive others of freewill through land-use controls — to create a politics of beauty?

Such aesthetic questions are, of course, ageless, and I can not pretend to be another Plato, Kant, Burke, Santayana, or Dewey. But professing humility doesn't quash my desire to know, no more than I can pretend not to have shared the nation's curiosity about the ultimate verdict in the O.J. Simpson trial or any newsy unsolved mystery. And no more than recognizing the scientific fact of mortality lessens my own wish not to die.

Despite her pain that long, suffering summer, my mother, too, never wished to die. But she knew she was about to die, she didn't have to tell me. What she wanted, she said with ever more vigor during her last few days of living, was "to get out of this hospital and go back home." The doctors told me that was not possible; so instead of taking her home, I talked about home, about the world and its weather outside her hospital room, about the view from Ashby's Gap that day. The only view she had was through her hospital window, much too narrow in fact to offer much of a view at all, with the outside landscape segmented into perfectly straight, horizontal lines of Venetian-blind plastic. When her eyes were closed, as they often were when I talked about Ashby's Gap, she could see much better, much farther, I'm sure.

Of that day's weather, the way it played on the landscape, the filters and angles of light it provided, the sky's colors, she knew nothing. All she knew came through the Weather Channel, to which her room's television was constantly set. She never asked that the channel be changed. Instead, she always asked me about "the weird weather we've been having." About the heavy rains and flood in June that washed out bridges and carried away cars and houses on the eastern slope of the Blue Ridge, just south of Ashby's Gap. About the unusually severe drought that followed, all through July well into August, turning the normally lush Piedmont brown. The weather was something to talk about, to fill the awkward silences, to avoid talking about what we feared. But it was far from idle chit-chat, I think. The weather held out meaning and hope when there was none, something to hold onto, because by continuously changing, the bad could always get better. And more, I think, the weather served as a layered context of reference and significance for a 75-year-old woman who, though not a farmer herself at the mercy of weather's whimsy, had lived virtually all her days in a rural Piedmont county seat that derived its reason for being from agriculture.

If I tried to change the subject or the television channel to, say, the California courtroom drama that was being broadcast on just about every other station and into every other hospital room, my mother would just shake her head. She wasn't interested, wasn't curious anymore. She would, however, nod affirmatively and as vigorously as she could, now too weak to speak, whenever I would mention that I was trying to figure out a way to get her out of the hospital and take her home. Despite her doctors' opinion that she should absolutely stay put, I finally did discover a home-hospice nurse who said it was possible, indeed desirable, to take my mother home. We made arrangements for the next day; but my mother never made it home, for that very morning, at 3 a.m., she died alone. Three hours before the sun came up on the other, the eastern and morning, side of the Blue Ridge. The September day would be partly cloudy; the low temperature, 66 degrees.

Local papers in the Piedmont still don't print the cause of death in obituaries. Only if it's a news story, like that about the accident victim at Ashby's Gap, is it fit to print. But in a small town, everybody knows anyway. Or if they don't, they pry discreetly: "I didn't realize she was sick. She seemed so healthy." But to pinpoint the cause of death, particularly a previously undiagnosed terminal illness, is not as medically precise as we would no doubt like to believe. When did it start? Could it have been prevented? If it had been diagnosed earlier, would it have been curable? A wise doctor shakes his head, knowing that most often these questions are unanswerable — or, if

answered, serve no useful purpose.

No more useful than my learning the precise cause of the auto accident at Ashby's Gap. But is usefulness the only measure? Beauty, for example, may be transcendental, religious even, but is it useful? As many artists are more than happy to admit, their work, indeed all art, *does* nothing. We behold and appreciate beauty only when we have the time, when our bellies are full, when we don't *need* to do anything else. Beauty is not necessary for survival. Survival maybe, but life itself? Can there be a life without beauty?

There is yet another, almost medical, way of looking at beauty, too. (Do such purely scientific explanations satisfy? — that is another question.) The appreciation of beauty is in our genes, say the currently fashionable evolutionary biologists. The survival of the most beautiful (that is, those whose features are most symmetrical, showing their genes are fit): A pretty woman and a handsome man are more likely to mate and thus ensure the enduring life of the fittest genes.

But perhaps even more important is the survival of those most appreciative of beauty: A beautiful sunset got the attention of our long-ago ancestors, letting them prepare for dangers that would soon be lurking in the night. Conversely, a beautiful sunrise got our ancestors up and about, finding food and whatever else it took for them and their genetic offspring (ultimately us) to survive. And the beautiful view from Ashby's Gap? That, too, is in our genes. The well-watered, gently rolling pastures of the Piedmont stir ancient memories of the hospitable savannas where what we now think of as human life evolved. Moreover, enjoying informative views from hilltops provided Homo sapiens with a distinct survival advantage over our now extinct cousins, the Neanderthals, who preferred low-lying valleys.

It's an old land, these remnants of once great mountains that now form the Piedmont. And what one sees from Ashby's Gap does look reassuringly ageless. We will die, but the beauty we behold will not. And just as my mother's body is buried now in this rolling land that she called beautiful, so I like to think her consciousness lives in what Yeats, no doctor or scientist, called the "Great Memory" or *Spiritus Mundi*. Human beings have souls, in other words, as Virgil discovered in the spiritual landscape he called Arcadia, that classical Piedmont. Our souls join us timelessly together. Whether in our genes or learned from our parents, whether we know it or not, we appreciate, even worship, beauty. I know my mother did. Her church was the natural world. That's why we were put here on this earth — I remember her saying when I was young — to appreciate what God created. That's the true story, this story anyway, the story that the newspapers and CNN don't report, the news that stays news, even after we die. And because we do die, maybe it is the only story.

After my own death, when it comes, my children will no doubt sort through my personal belongings, as I have now done their grandmother's. Among the stacks of files and puzzling papers, perhaps they'll discover a yellowed, crumpled newspaper clipping about a fatal auto accident at Ashby's Gap. Why did our father keep this clipping? Who was this man, the driver of the car? What's the connection? What's the story here?

"I want to go to heaven," were the whispered, last words of my mother, according to the nurse on duty that early morning before the sun came up. It sounds now like a child's prayer, overheard by a parent. Had I, her only child, been with her then, I think she would have said instead, "I want to go home." On the way, we would have passed through Ashby's Gap. ❧

THE MONOTYPES IN *PIECES OF THE PIEDMONT*

AT its most basic form, a monotype is created by painting ink on a smooth surface, such as a metal or glass print plate, and pressing the plate and paper together. Most of the ink is transferred to the paper, and the result is a single, unique image. The process is popular with artists for its "low-tech" simplicity, directness, and the intimacy with which the viewer is connected with the printmaker and his intent.

Since 1985, printmaker Tucker Hill has been making monotype prints of the northern tier of the Virginia Piedmont centering on his home county of Madison. Like many other "outsiders," the native Richmonder was attracted to the region by its combination of picturesque vistas, distinct rolling landscape, and rural character.

Hill decided at the very beginning to restrict his recording of the Piedmont to the unique qualities of the monotype and, as an admirer of classic black and white photography, to restrict his "color" range to a mixture of black and burnt umber oil colors.

Hill begins gathering ideas for prints with long drives across the countryside, taking photographs and recording the time, date, and location, which later become the title for the print. Some ideas take time to find their way into creation, with the actual print date being years after the initial recording date.

Back home, Hill makes detailed study sketches of the scene, inspired by the photographs. On the date of the printing, a final sketch is made on tracing paper, which is placed on a light table, and a clear acrylic print plate is placed over the sketch. Using the sketch as a guide, ink is manipulated on the plate using various brushes, sharp points, Q-Tips— anything to achieve the effect.

The inking of the print plate must be done in a single day, non-stop before it dries. The inked plate is placed on the bed of an etching press, covered by a sheet of damp print paper, and run through the press. The ink is transferred to the paper, and a monotype is the result.

Cover:
Old Rag Mountain, Route 644, Madison County, May 1, 1994 (Printed January 26, 1996).

Town of Etlan, Route 231, Madison County, December 1991 (Printed December 29, 1991).

Foreword
Route 643, Madison County, August 10, 1991, 6:45 p.m. (Printed January 28, 1996).

page 6
South River Valley and Saddleback Mountain, Route 637, Greene County, January 1, 1990, 4:23 p.m. (Printed January 7, 1990).